What is Freedom? Is it for You?

25 IDEAS THAT WILL CHANGE THE WAY YOU SEE AMERICA!

By Shane F. Krauser

In liberty,

[signature]

ISBN: 978-0-9850540-2-1
What is Freedom? Is it for You?
25 Ideas That Will Change the Way You See America!
Published by SK Publications in Chandler, Arizona

Cover design and typesetting by Ralph Richardson
Edited by Barrett Tillman and Don Petrie

For more information, contact info@ShaneKrauser.com.

Printed and bound in the United States of America

For wholesale and bulk discounts for educational, business, fundraising, and sales promotional use, contact info@ShaneKrauser.com.

Dedication

This book is dedicated to my heroes,
namely our founding fathers.

They pledged to each other their lives,
their fortunes, and their sacred honor,
and this book is an attempt to awaken
their spirit within every American
who wishes to see and experience
the America that the founders
originally envisioned.

The text of the U.S. Constitution and the Declaration of Independence came from the Federal Government Archives website.

Table of Contents

Foreword

Anyone who has ever attempted a do-it-yourself home-improvement project knows what it is like to search for just the right tool. What at first appeared as an easy task quickly turned difficult because, without the correct tool, proceeding further was nearly impossible. However, once that perfect wrench or ratchet and socket was found, things proceeded smoothly to conclusion.

Understanding, appreciating, and then preserving freedom in America is very similar. When first exposed to the concept of freedom, the task of keeping it and passing it along to the next generation seems so simple as to be ridiculous. But when one digs deeper and discovers just how fragile and rare true freedom is in society, and how its very existence is under attack from almost all sides, it is easy to become overwhelmed with the enormity of the job. We grasp for ideas on what can be done, we fumble around like we've got ten thumbs when trying to discuss the principles and issues with friends and neighbors, and ultimately we get no further than scattered pieces on the floor with no directions in sight. And ultimately, we wonder if we can really make a difference at all. Is it a project we can even complete?

Enter Shane Krauser. His latest book is like a well stocked and ordered toolbox with just the right tool at hand immediately available for the tasks required. Whether this is your first book on the subject of freedom, or your one-hundredth, you will find it to fit snugly in your hand and be immediately applicable to the project of understanding and preserving freedom in your country. It's comprehensive reach but brief handling of each of the key components of freedom make it a very readable book, and very useful as well. It is a really a shorthand approach to master-level understanding.

In our busy lives, we need just such a tool to be able to cut through the clutter and know exactly what we need to know. Shane Krauser is very economical in his prose and doesn't lose the reader on flights of fancy. Freedom is much too important a topic to be written about for the sake of the vanity of the author. This is yet another feature of this book I appreciate. Shane handles the subject with the directness and seriousness that it deserves, as if we don't have time to lose. And quite frankly, we don't. Freedom is in danger. However, Shane balances this well, also, avoiding the alarmism that can sometimes ruin otherwise good information.

So roll up your sleeves and get started on a project that is not only worthy of your time, but also crucial to your future. This book is exactly the right tool for the job.

Chris Brady
NY Times bestselling author
CEO Life Leadership

Preface

Imagine you are in an airplane preparing for take off, and you are lucky enough to talk with the pilot as you prepare for departure. You ask him how long he has been a pilot, and he responds that this is his first flight. You ask him if he has reviewed the checklist, and he boldly proclaims that he hasn't but he will if he experiences any problems in the air.

There is little question that you would not fly with such a pilot. And if we would not allow a pilot to fly an airplane without adherence to, or even a review of, the checklist prior to takeoff, why would we let people lead our nation without a working knowledge of our checklist, namely the Constitution? This is precisely what is happening in America.

We wouldn't allow a plumber to perform a knee replacement. We wouldn't seek out legal advice from a chef. We wouldn't hire an accountant to take care of our car's engine overhaul. So, why then, do we elect people to lead a nation who have no idea how to govern, what it means to be free, and what the Constitution actually requires? Why do we elect and reelect people who constantly violate their oaths of office?

If America is to be saved, it will be the result of individuals, with their families, neighbors, friends, and acquaintances, uniting in the framework of the Constitution and its overarching principles of freedom. This will require the people to learn about and embrace not only civic education but political action as well. One cannot defend freedom if there is no knowledge about the structure upon which freedom is best preserved. And one cannot rebuild a country if there is no understanding of the historical roots and influences that led to the building of the country in the first place. We cannot truly recognize and defeat bad government unless we first understand what good government looks like.

This volume is written and formatted to assist every individual to learn about the basic principles upon which America was founded and then incorporate them as we deal with the more detail-oriented problems that we, as a country, face today.

Indeed, the principles embodied in the Constitution are timeless, whether we choose to embrace them or not. The parchment document is of little relevance if it is not understood and enforced. It is the purpose—and the defense thereof—that holds real value.

The American people cannot demand that their representatives defend the principles of freedom that we, ourselves, do not understand and value. If our leaders continue to move our nation in the direction we have been heading over the last century, *it will be because we have allowed them to do so.*

We must stand together and recognize what is at stake. The current political framework is designed to divide the American political system into two opposing sides. The political machines have trained their support system to lobby against, to blame, and to resent, judge, and vilify the opposing view. The framework is designed to remove our individual identity, to eliminate accountability from our party's actions, to destroy the identity of the various states that are intricately tied with the people, and to centralize political power to the leadership of either side.

In the midst of this struggle, how is the individual to be represented? Are our rights as a free people subject to the whims of whatever majority or political party has risen to power? Of course not.

As Benjamin Franklin said to the lady who asked what the delegates of the Philadelphia Convention had given the American people, "A republic if you can keep it." In other words, we should not look, as a first priority, to our political leaders for answers. We must look to ourselves. And as we evolve into an educated populace, we will see significant change in our culture. Why? Because those in government are nothing more than a direct reflection of the values of the people. What we stand for as a culture is typically mirrored in the actions of those whom we elect.

When the citizenry cares less about freedom, tyranny will result because where there is no accountability revolving around the paradigm of freedom. Carte blanche to exercise unlimited power is the result. On the other hand, when a society establishes freedom as a first priority, liberty and even prosperity will spring forth.

As we take a journey down freedom's trail, you will be equipped with the tools needed to strengthen your own resolve and to educate others within your sphere of influence. You will understand the solutions and become an advocate for one of the greatest causes the world has ever known. To be effective, we have to strategize and then fight.

So, what if we could begin to engage the culture in a way that is non-political and revolves around the desire of most human beings to choose how they live their lives? What if we could come up with a series of questions designed to open the door to real discussion that could motivate a cultural awakening? There is a way. We simply have to begin asking questions that bring us together in our desire for liberty. We have to access the right tools.

As you get started, think about the following questions and consider placing them in your toolbox in the fight for liberty.

- Who wants to be told what to do?

- Who believes that government should follow the rules?

- Who believes that we should be able to keep the fruits of our labor?

Now, let's explore each question individually.

1. Who wants to be told what do?

No one wants to be told what to do. However, we have created a government that impacts virtually every area of our lives. Of course, we want government to intervene in order to protect our life, liberty, and property. However, people often endorse the idea of more freedom for them but then have no problem approving of government intervention against others and their liberties. We must remind others that the underlying philosophy of being left alone must apply consistently to all and not simply to a select few. To allow some to be free from government intervention while others are oppressed is antithetical to what it means to live in a free society.

2. Who believes that government should follow the rules?

We all believe that the government should follow the rules. The bigger question is which rules it should have to follow. The U.S. Constitution is the supreme law of the land until it is amended or replaced with something else. That has not happened. As a result, it is the rulebook.

3. Who believes that we should be able to keep the fruits of our labor?

Who doesn't believe they should be able to keep the fruits of their labor? Most people don't have an issue with this principle. The primary issue is when some feel that others have more. In a free society, no man has a right to take from another simply because someone has significantly more. Ironically, Americans—even poor Americans—have significantly more than the rest of the world. Even those people who say that those who have more should give to those who have less would not give of their own possessions to satisfy that philosophy. In other words, this is an empty, disproven idea—pie in the sky—and not something that most are willing to adhere to during their day-to-day lives.

Imagine being able to start discussions by utilizing these

three questions. More importantly, imagine educating those around you and being instrumental in the cause of freedom's restoration. This is just a glimpse of what you will experience in the coming pages.

Ultimately, we have an obligation. We must rise up to understand more, advocate more, and defend more. The future of our freedom is depending on it. As Thomas Jefferson said, we cannot experience ignorance and freedom simultaneously. We must understand, retain, and implement that which is our birthright, namely freedom. We must remain vigilant if we wish to relish in freedom. Here is our opportunity. It is our liberty and the liberty of future generations that is at stake. It is ours to preserve and defend.

So, what is freedom anyways and is it for you? It's time to explore tha answers to those questions together.

How to Use This Book

This book is designed to help you understand the "idea" of America, from the basic first principles to some of the more complicated philosophies. Each chapter is designed to teach you and then teach you how to teach others. The hope is that this book will be used around the dinner table, neighborhood discussions, grassroots focus groups, churches of every denomination, political dialogue, and in our schools.

Each chapter deals with a particular subject. First, you'll experience an explanation of the subject. After each explanation, you will see an area entitled "Lesson" and "Discussion Questions."

The "Lesson" is designed to facilitate some ways to teach these ideas. Be creative and think outside the box when considering ways to solidify these ideas in the participants' minds and hearts.

The "Discussion Questions" are given as an illustration of questions that can be asked. Many of them are informational. Others are designed to facilitate a debate. From these questions, you should expound on other ideas that come to your mind, as they no doubt will.

This is our time to defend liberty. We must reignite the principles of freedom, see America for what she is, and defend her by pledging our lives, our fortunes, and our sacred honor. This is where it all begins. Let's get to work.

Chapter 1
What is Freedom?

"Education is favorable to liberty. Freedom can only exist in a society of knowledge. Without learning, men are incapable of knowing their rights. And where learning is confined to a few people, ... liberty can neither be equal nor universal."
~Dr. Benjamin Rush, 1786

The Declaration of Independence declares that every person is endowed by their Creator with certain unalienable rights. Every person, simply by virtue of that person's humanity, is born with fundamental liberties and freedoms. No person, elected representative, or piece of paper grants these rights. They are inherent in every human being.

You have the right to think what you wish, say what you think, and write what you say. You have the right to keep those things that you earn through your own productivity and by the sweat of your brow. You have the right to acquire, enjoy, and dispose of your own property. You have the right to be left alone inside your own home, the right to travel, the right to associate with whom you wish, and the right to defend yourself and your family. The list goes on and on.

Freedom is the ability to do what one wishes with those inherent rights so long as it does not infringe on the rights of other individuals. For example, while you have the right to speak, you do not have the right to use that speech to incite a riot or to yell "fire" in a crowded theater that is not on fire. Why? Because of the direct and non-consensual harm that may be caused to other people as a result of your actions. Freedom used in a way that causes harm to others is where your freedom ends. Freedom and responsibility, indeed, go hand in hand.

While we often focus on the idea that freedom revolves

around our personal desires and pursuits, freedom also means that people have the obligation to behave responsibly to protect and preserve their own liberty and the liberties of others. When our neighbor's freedoms are attacked, it should be considered an attack on the freedoms of everyone.

Freedom is difficult to maintain and requires absolute vigilance. Why? Because freedom is often taken from the people by those who govern or even the majority of people under the guise of public safety, social justice, or even fairness. As Benjamin Franklin said, "He that would trade liberty for security deserves neither."

In any society that wishes to experience freedom, the people must agree to take the risk that certain harm or ideas that the majority disagrees with may find their way into their culture. No society can offer its members an environment of liberty without some degree of risk. Risks are an inherent part of life. The issue is simply whether we will allow risks and call ourselves free or eliminate all risks using the arm of government and simply wonder what it's like to be free. In other words, are we willing to ignore the counsel of Benjamin Franklin and trade our "liberty for security"?

Consider the following: In a free society, we allow people to speak their opinions even though they may disagree with our own. We allow people to own and possess firearms even though some people may behave irresponsibly with such a right. We allow people to participate and watch circuses and airplane aerobatics even though harm may result to the participants or even the viewers. We allow people to skydive and rock climb, even if some of the risks are perceived as rather serious. Even in light of these dangers, a society that claims to be free must be willing to accept these risks. A free society prides itself on not posting red tape every time someone is harmed by his own actions or the actions of another who may have taken an unreasonable risk or used their own pursuit of happiness in a way that carried a heavier risk than what others might take.

If a society cannot accept that sometimes unfortunate incidents happen and is willing to trade liberty for the promise of "no risk," the people will eventually find themselves living under tyrannical rule where freedom is secondary to the supposed interests of the majority or those who govern.

The essence of freedom is the fact that all people are free and should be protected as such even if the majority of the population disagrees with the practices of one particular person or group. Freedom is the ability of individuals to practice and exercise their own liberties so long as the exercise of those freedoms does not infringe on the freedoms of others.

So, what is freedom and is it for you? Societies have struggled for centuries with this concept. As we're learning, it's freedom that is rather simple. It's tyranny that is complicated.

Lesson

1. In your group, tell everyone that you will be conducting the meeting. As you begin, tell people where they will sit, which direction they will face, and what they may or may not say. Tell them to take off their shoes, take control of their property, and then disperse these items as you see fit. As people laugh, tell them laughter is not permitted. If people in the group have brought things with them, take those things and pile them up in one area of the room and tell them you will decide if and when this property will be returned. Engage in a discussion with the group. As they make comments, tell them they are wrong, misinformed, or uninformed and explain to them what you actually perceive as the truth. Make absurd and obnoxious claims in response to the participants' statements. After conducting this exercise, engage in a discussion of what it really means to be free and the dangers of one man or a group interfering with one's freedom.

2. Imagine hundreds of people gather at an outdoor arena to watch aerobatic airplanes perform. At one point, an airplane loses control and crashes into the crowd killing scores of individuals. Discuss what the appropriate governmental response should be, if any. Should we ban these sorts of aerobatic shows because the risk is too high? Why or why not? Should government create tougher regulations to ensure that this sort of tragedy does not happen again? As you engage in this discussion, share the following: A former airline pilot quoted a passenger who said anything is justified "if it saves just one life." The pilot said, "First, flying will never be 100% safe, and if it could be, nobody could afford it." Are we legislating freedom out of existence?

3. Debate: Our freedom to act does not include the freedom to hurt other people. Does "harm" include just physical harm or does it also include financial, emotional, and psychological harm? If it includes something other than physical harm, how do we measure injury?

Discussion Questions

1. What does it mean to be free?

2. What do you think are the greatest dangers to freedom?

3. Are there limitations on freedom? If so, what are those limitations and how far should they be extended?

4. How can a society best protect freedom? What is your individual obligation?

5. Why is freedom a risky proposition? What dangers does a free society often experience?

Chapter 2
Defending the Rights of All

"He that would make his own liberty secure,
must guard even his enemy from oppression."
~Thomas Paine

Consider the following: On Monday, your neighbor steals your bike, and, on Tuesday, your neighbor stands in front of the local courthouse and hops on one leg and whistles "Dixie." "Dixie" happens to be a song you absolutely despise.

Would you seek to punish both acts? Of course you wouldn't. You would seek punishment for the theft of your bike because your neighbor deprived you of your property. However, you wouldn't seek to punish an individual simply because they engage in annoying, distasteful, or ridiculous habits or make certain choices with which you disagree. If a person chooses to hop on one leg and whistle, he is hurting no one in the truest sense of "injury." If someone steals your property, that is an infringement on your right to acquire and possess property.

All human beings are born to be free and to make their own decisions without government interference. In addition, their choices cannot be infringed upon simply because the majority disagrees with such choices. Of course, if a person makes a decision that hurts another individual, like injuring, killing another person, or damaging another's property, consequences may be appropriate.

However, what happens when you simply don't like the actions of your neighbor or you believe that society should adopt certain policies to ensure we are healthier as a people? What should we do if our actions are not hurting anyone or interfering with anyone else's liberty or freedom? The answer is that we must defend the rights of others to behave in ways we may not agree with, so long as those actions are

5

not harming anyone else, and then engage in the contest of ideas to engage others about the ideas with which we may disagree.

For example, you may not like the fact that one chooses to eat caramel apples and chocolate for breakfast, grease-filled burgers and deep-fried Twinkies for lunch, and ice cream and bacon-wrapped pretzel dogs for dinner, but is this a choice that we, as a society, should eliminate by way of legislation? No! When one begins to regulate certain choices, our own choices will ultimately be threatened by that same body seeking to restrict our choices simply because someone else disagrees with them. It's a vicious cycle perpetuated by those who feel they must impose their own value judgments on others.

Listen in to the following conversation about freedom of speech between a father and his freedom-fighting son, Daniel.

Father: A group is gathering downtown to advocate a message that is absolutely contemptible. Let's shut them down!

Danie: I disagree, Dad. Let them speak.

Father: What? Why would you even contemplate defending certain people who engage in despicable speech?

Daniel: Because I don't want to be a slave.

Father: A slave? What does this have to do with slavery?

Daniel: Simple. If you choose not to protect ideas you find despicable, who will stand with you when your ideas are deemed despicable? A failure to stand for the freedom of others means ultimate slavery for us all.

Father: So, aren't you endorsing their behavior by doing so?

Daniel: Of course not. I can disagree with their ideas, engage them about the problems with their ideas, and still protect their freedom to participate in their contemptible speech. What do you prefer: market forces or government force? If you prefer freedom, we better vigorously protect the market place of ideas.

Daniel is absolutely right. Responsible people recognize that the issue does not end with simply protecting the liberties of others. We should not make laws that stop people from making choices that arguably may harm only themselves and no one else. However, in a society that is constantly trying to improve, we should be a voice for good and, with power, persuasion, and credibility, illustrate why certain choices should or should not be made.

There is a significant difference between forcing someone to do something by way of a law or edict and allowing people to be accountable for their own decisions while learning about the negative consequences of such decisions through their own experience and/or the marketplace of ideas. The former is tantamount to tyranny, while the latter is fundamental to the idea of freedom.

Lesson

1. Discover something that everyone in the group agrees is potentially unhealthy but delicious nonetheless. For example, fast food hamburgers, bacon, or soda drinks. As you do this, consider going somewhere or simply staying home. Enjoy a healthy meal intermingled with a tinge of unhealthiness. As you enjoy the meal or snack, ask who would be in favor of making a law outlawing the consumption of these items. Of course, people will likely disagree that such a law should be made because "It's my choice. And besides, it's tasty!"

   Before you move to the next component of the lesson, you must plan to have someone who is prepared to argue against the entire group. For example, let's assume the majority in the group don't drink alcohol or eat red meat. Propose a law that would ban alcohol or red meat because it is, from the group's perspective, unhealthy. You will want to have your "plant" adamantly argue that "I don't consume those items so any legislation prohibiting consumption won't affect me. Besides, it is unhealthy. Let's make a law."

The debate will take on a life of its own as you discuss which laws are appropriate and which are not. The point that needs to be made is that we protect the rights of everyone to choose how much soda they want to drink, how many Big Macs they will consume at one sitting, and whether they will drink five cups of coffee daily. We protect the rights of everyone because, when we do so, we are protecting our own ability to choose. We do not want the majority making the decisions as to how all of us will lead our lives. We also do not want the government condoning behavior as acceptable which often creates a moral hazard and reduces the incentives for people to use their own judgment.

2. Debate the following scenario in order to understand the importance of defending the liberties of others.

Imagine that a group shows up in your town and protests on the sidewalk of your downtown area. The protesters do not obstruct traffic, and their demonstration is peaceful. However, the ideas that they promote are reprehensible, and some people are offended, outraged, and even begin acting out towards the protestors. As you debate, throw in any topic that this group is advocating (e.g., racial supremacy, misogyny, hatred towards those who serve in the military, flag burning, etc.). As this group protests, the police show up to shut it down due to several complaints. What are the advantages of standing up and defending their "right" to say what they wish even if you disagree with the nature of the action? Disadvantages?

Discussion Questions

1. Why must we protect the rights of those with whom we disagree?

2. What is the danger of allowing government to outlaw things we do not like or care about so long as those things that we appreciate are protected?

3. How have societies failed where people were not allowed to be free? What was the result?

4. Why must we be educated as to liberty and freedom? What are the dangers of remaining ignorant in these areas?

5. How do we create a culture that truly understands freedom and that reciprocally respects the freedom of everyone? How might tools found through media outlets, social media, churches, schools, etc. be instrumental in creating this result?

Chapter 3
Tyranny in the American Colonies and the Response

"When the people fear the government, there is tyranny, when the government fears the people, there is liberty."
~Thomas Jefferson

Now that we've experienced the general proposition surrounding the concept of freedom, let's evaluate the response of the founding generation to a perceived attack on their freedom. The founders experienced tyranny and oppression by a government that disregarded their fundamental liberties. In this chapter, you will get a glimpse of a few of the things they experienced. As you read the following, imagine what you might do under the same circumstances.

From 1754 to 1763, England battled France on the American continent. As a result of the French and Indian war, England began to evolve into a military super power. England incurred incredible debt and, as a result, began enacting laws both to control and collect money from the colonists. Ultimately, England's oppressive actions angered the colonists.

In 1763, there were thirteen colonies along the Atlantic seaboard. For more than 150 years, many of the colonists sought and secured land and relished in the results of hard work and personal productivity.

In 1763, England issued a proclamation restricting westward expansion beyond the Allegheny Mountains. George Washington was particularly concerned about this proclamation since he owned 40,000 acres west of the area declared off-limits. Not only did the rule concern Washington, it justifiably angered the colonists because they felt that England was trying to control their movement and, thus, their freedom. In fact, England sent over 10,000 troops to ensure that the colonists did not violate the order.

In 1764, England passed a slightly modified version of the 1733 Sugar and Molasses Act, which was about to expire. Under the Sugar Act, colonial merchants were required to pay a tax on the importation of molasses, among other goods. However, the colonists generally evaded the 1733 legislation. But in 1764, England became more aggressive in the collection of taxes by increasing customs enforcement.

While the Sugar Act reduced the tax on molasses, enforcement was enhanced and the act listed additional goods to be taxed, including sugar, certain wines, coffee, pimiento, cambric, and printed calico. It also regulated the export of iron and lumber. The consequences of these taxes disrupted the colonial economy by reducing the foreign markets to which the colonies could sell their goods, and the amount of currency available to them for the purchase of British manufactured goods. The act enflamed the anger that the colonists felt toward England.

The colonists' anger amplified when, in 1765, England passed the Quartering Act, which mandated that the colonists provide barracks, supplies, and food for British troops. The colonists recognized that people cannot and should not be forced to use their property in such a way to meet the demands of government without their consent. Take a look at the Third Amendment, which addresses the quartering of soldiers, and you'll understand why this amendment even exists.

In 1765, England also passed the Stamp Act, a direct tax that required colonists to pay taxes and acquire a stamp (which incidentally bore the image of the king) for all legal documents, playing cards, contracts, lease agreements, and even posters to be hung on a tree. This tax only applied to those living in the colonies. It did not apply to those living in the motherland of England, which infuriated the colonists.

Again, the imposition of this tax angered many, although others, like Benjamin Franklin who was in England at the time, believed it was a mere aberration and would pass with time. He even tried to secure a job for one of his nephews to work as a stamp collector. However, Franklin soon realized that the colonists were disturbed by yet another tax imposed by the Crown without the consent of the colonists. It wouldn't be much longer before people like Franklin would join the resistance to England's overreach.

As a result of the outcry of the colonists, the British Parliament agreed to repeal the Stamp Act on the condition that the Declaratory Act, which stated that Parliament had the authority to enact laws that were binding on the colonies, was passed. Thus, on March 18, 1766, the Parliament repealed the Stamp Act and passed the Declaratory Act. Essentially, England did not buy the "taxation without representation" argument and asserted that it could legislate for the colonies in "all cases whatsoever." It was a bit like saying, "You can do whatever you want, just don't do what we disapprove of." To the colonists, enacting the Declaratory Act was yet another proverbial slap in the face, and tension among the colonists continued to mount.

In 1767, England imposed yet more taxes through the Townsend Act, which taxed tea, paint, paper, glass, etc. England knew that these various items could, for the most part, only be obtained from overseas, thus making the payment of this tax a virtual impossibility.

In 1768, the colonists who were on the front lines of the taxation battle wanted to give their own people an ultimatum and force them to take sides. The Boston merchants drafted the Non-Importation Agreement, which encouraged colonists not to trade with British merchants. This was monumental, as one could, with time, identify who was a Loyalist (sided with the British) and who was a Patriot (sided with those opposed to the actions taken by the British government). For example, if a person was seen wearing "homespun" clothing, it was likely that person was a Patriot, as finer clothing and linen were usually obtained from overseas. The colonists were beginning to tighten the noose on both English tyranny and any apathetic colonists.

In 1773, England engaged in yet another disturbing "taxing" maneuver by passing the Tea Act. While tea was already subject to a tax, England made it clear that the "Tea Act" would subject the colonists to additional and ongoing taxes which, in part, would assist in bailing out the financially-troubled British East India Company. More importantly, the Tea Act gave the East India Company a monopoly on the sale of tea in the colonies, which infringed on the basic notions of freedom and the free enterprise system of the colonists.

In December of 1773, the anger of many of the colonists culminated in Boston Harbor where they tossed about 10,000 pounds of tea into the water. The action was tantamount to a declaration of war and became known as the Boston Tea Party. The colonists opposed to the policies and laws imposed on them by England did not necessarily inflict physically harm on anyone. Instead, they destroyed property—an interesting strategy that would facilitate the revolution.

In response to the Boston Tea Party, England passed several new laws in 1774. The Administration of Justice Act mandated that any charges brought against British personnel be handled in areas outside of the colonies. George Washington referred to this as the "Murder Act" because individuals who were not tried in the colonies would likely never be brought to justice. The Massachusetts Government Act replaced all of the colonist's government officials with officials appointed by England. Finally, the Boston Port Act closed down Boston Harbor until the colonists repaid the East India Tea Company for the damaged tea. In addition, the tax on the damaged tea would have to be paid.

The rancor among the colonists caused by England's laws

and taxation finally rose to the point at which the colonists recognized that a critical choice had to be made: either submit and be a subject of the Crown or resist and be free. The former would require no real sacrifice. The latter would imperil the lives, the fortunes, and the sacred honor of those patriots who would choose freedom and liberty over servitude.

Lesson

1. Exercise caution when moving forward with this lesson. Access a large rat trap. Yes, a real rat trap. Illustrate how powerful the trap is by taking a pencil and observe the trap literally snap it in half. Allow others to participate and comment on the violence of this trap and what it is designed to do. Engage the trap once again and allow everyone to see you place it in a bag. Ask for a volunteer and have him come to the front and face the crowd. As your volunteer faces the crowd, disengage the trap (while your volunteer is looking away) and ask the participant whether he is willing to put his hand into the bag. The hope is that he will put his hand into the bag where a treat (e.g., a candy bar, etc.) will be waiting for him. Talk about the fact that we must be willing to engage those who would undermine freedom, and it will not be easy. However, preserving freedom is not just our duty. It is a joy, a privilege, and a sacred honor.

2. Debate: Were other alternatives available to the colonists? Was war the last resort? At what point are the people justified in waging war and engaging in conflict to defend liberty?

3. Illustration of excessive taxation: Tell the following story and engage in a discussion. If a person arrived on your doorstep, threatened you if you did not give up your money, and you ultimately gave up your property, the crime of robbery has occurred. Now, what if the person at the door was a government official who was there to

collect taxes and threatened to put you in jail if you did not give up your money for purposes of paying your "fair share"? What is the difference between the two scenarios? For what purposes should government be able to collect taxes, and at what point is resistance permissible? What would the founders have said?

Discussion Questions

1. During the 1760s and 1770s, the colonists were experiencing about a 2-3% tax burden. Why were they willing to rise up and literally pledge their lives to the cause of opposing the taxation policies?

2. What does "taxation without representation" mean? Why were the colonists so upset by this action?

3. Why should the people be represented in the government process as opposed to allowing a king to make all of the decisions without consulting the people and their representatives?

4. What happens when people refuse to protect those things that are precious? Is it possible to recover freedom once it is lost? Consider the quote by John Q. Adams: "Liberty, once lost, is lost forever."

5. Under what circumstances should the people pay taxes and what should that money be used for? How much of one's income or worth should the people have to give to the government?

6. Are we dealing with a "taxation without representation" issue in America today? If so, what are the remedies?

7. England attempted to bail out the East India Tea Company. Is government ever justified in providing taxpayer resources to private businesses? Explain.

Chapter 4
Let Freedom Ring:
The Declaration of Independence

"If ye love wealth better than liberty, the tranquility of servitude better than the animating contest of freedom, go home from us in peace. We ask not your counsels or arms. Crouch down and lick the hands which feed you. May your chains set lightly upon you, and may posterity forget that ye were our countrymen."
~Samuel Adams

As the British government exerted its authority, the colonists' efforts were relatively ineffective. In 1774 in Philadelphia, Pennsylvania, the First Continental Congress convened. While some of the founders wished to declare independence at that point, most agreed to give England one last chance. They issued to England the Declaration of Rights and Grievances which reiterated the fundamental rights of man, the function of government, and the importance of integrity among those who govern.

The English government rejected the Declaration outright, and, recognizing that resistance was building, King George III noted to Lord North that "blows must decide whether they are to be subject to this country or independent." The colonists had some critical decisions to make, and it certainly wouldn't be easy.

On June 19, 1775, the Second Continental Congress convened, and George Washington was appointed the General of the Continental Army. The American Revolution had begun, and Washington and his army found themselves continually on the run.

As a result of the Second Continental Congress, our founders recognized the importance of issuing a declaration of human rights for all the world to see. The American colonies had been at war with Britain for nearly a year, and the colonists had to decide upon their strategy and the ultimate execution of that strategy.

On June 7, 1776, Richard Henry Lee moved Congress to adopt the resolution that the colonies are, and of right ought to be, free and independent states. Of course, during this time, the Continental Congress was having to deal with some critical choices facing the most powerful military in the world. As a result, Congress would table Lee's resolution. However, in anticipation of the vote, Congress selected a committee of five to draft a declaration of independence. Yes, the writing was on the wall and the fight for independence was imminent.

The Committee of Five consisted of Benjamin Franklin, Thomas Jefferson, John Adams, Roger Sherman, and Robert Livingston. Of the five, Benjamin Franklin was first asked to write the declaration. However, he refused seemingly because he did not want to author something that would be subject to revision.

Thomas Jefferson and John Adams were at odds as to who should write the document between the two of them. John Adams finally set the record straight by outlining the following to Thomas Jefferson:

"Reason first: You are a Virginian and a Virginian ought to appear at the head of this business. Reason second: I am obnoxious, suspected and unpopular. You are very much otherwise. Reason third: You can write ten times better than I can."

Thomas Jefferson ultimately accepted the challenge to write the document. On June 11, 1776, Jefferson began writing, and it took him a mere 17 days. On June 28, he submitted the draft to Congress, and, for several days, the delegates worked through and edited the document.

On July 2, 1776, the Continental Congress formally adopted

the Declaration of Independence, and, on July 4, 1776, it was formally declared to the public, and the world was now on notice as to the position of the colonists. John Hancock was the president of the Continental Congress and would sign the Declaration of Independence. However, most of the signers would put their hand to the document beginning in August 1776.

The purpose of the Declaration of Independence was two fold:

1. To recognize the nature of man and the fact that man is born with inherent freedoms.

2. To provide justification to the world for the American colonists going to war against England.

Here are some of the key features of the Declaration of Independence. As you review them, notice that Jefferson recognizes some key components regarding man, power, freedom, the purpose of government, and the justification for revolution. This is a wonderfully and beautifully written document.

Source of Political Independence – "When in the Course of human events, it becomes necessary for one people to dissolve the political bands which have connected them with another, and to assume among the powers of the earth, the separate and equal station to which the Laws of Nature and of Nature's God entitle them, a decent respect to the opinions of mankind requires that they should declare the causes which impel them to the separation."

Philosophy of Government – "We hold these truths to be self-evident, that all men are created equal, that they are endowed by their Creator with certain unalienable Rights, that among these are Life, Liberty and the pursuit of Happiness."

Purpose of Government – "That to secure these rights [life, liberty, and the pursuit of happiness], Governments are instituted among Men, . . ."

Popular Sovereignty – "...deriving their just powers from the consent of the governed, ..."

Authority for Government Reform – "That whenever any Form of Government becomes destructive of these ends, it is the Right of the People to alter or to abolish it, and to institute new Government, laying its foundation on such principles and organizing its powers in such form, as to them shall seem most likely to effect their Safety and Happiness."

Lack of Action is Typical of the Governed - "...all experience hath shewn, that mankind are more disposed to suffer, while evils are sufferable, than to right themselves by abolishing the forms to which they are accustomed.

Justification for Government Reform – "But when a long train of abuses and usurpations, pursuing invariably the same Object evinces a design to reduce them under absolute Despotism, it is their right, it is their duty, to throw off such Government, and to provide new Guards for their future security."

Supporting Documentation or Indictment of Abuses (Total of 27 listed) – "The history of the present King of Great Britain is a history of repeated injuries and usurpations, all having in direct object the establishment of an absolute Tyranny over these States. To prove this, let Facts be submitted to a candid world."

Abuses 1-12 (Tyranny v. Representative Government)

The abuses initially listed in the Declaration involved King George III's establishment of tyranny in lieu of a representative government. The foundation of representative government is the power of the people to exercise their voice and collectively make laws for the public good. King George III was a tyrant in almost every aspect of his rule over the colonies.

He unequivocally interfered with that process by rejecting legislation proposed by the colonies. He dissolved colonial bodies of representation, replaced colonial governments with his appointed ministers, and interfered with the naturalization of citizens in new regions. He extended his tyrannical control by interrupting the objective judicial processes and abridging the civil rights of the colonists. He prevented the exercise of judicial powers in the colonies and made judges dependent on him for their jobs and salaries. He also established tyrannical control over the colonies by maintaining a strong military presence. And, worse yet, he kept standing armies in the colonies during a time of peace, made the military power superior to the civil government, and forced the colonists to support the military presence through increased taxation schemes.

Abuses 13-22 (Destruction of Self-Rule)

This next list of abuses describes the involvement of Parliament in destroying the colonists' right to self-rule. King George III "combined with others" to subject the colonists to legislation passed without colonial input or the colonists' consent. Legislation required the colonists to quarter English troops in their homes, terminated trade with other parts of the world, imposed taxes without the consent of colonial legislatures, eliminated the right to trial by jury, and compelled colonists to be tried in England. In addition, legislation established absolute rule throughout the colonies, removed the authority of colonial governments, and forbade any legislative action by the colonial governments.

Abuses 23-27 (Specific Actions by King George)

The final list of abuses refers to specific actions that King George III took to wage war against the colonies. He attempted to suppress the colonial rebellion through violence and unmitigated military force. He directed the British military to attack colonists, burn their towns to the ground, attack their ships, and destroy the livelihood of the people. He hired foreign mercenaries to fight against the colonies.

He kidnapped American sailors to force them into British military service, refused to protect the colonies from Indian attack, and created division and caused the colonists to fight against each other.

Denunciation

The Declaration of Independence concludes by expressing the ideal for which they were willing to fight, essentially recognizing that where there is tyranny, the people cannot be free.

"In every stage of these Oppressions We have Petitioned for Redress in the most humble terms: Our repeated Petitions have been answered only by repeated injury. A Prince, whose character is thus marked by every act which may define a Tyrant, is unfit to be the ruler of a free people."

The final piece was now in place through the publication, and commitment to, the Declaration of Independence. Now all that was needed to secure that independence was to defeat the most powerful military in the world.

Lesson

1. Read the Declaration of Independence in Appendix A. Name three of the grievances outlined by Thomas Jefferson and discuss why the founders percevied them as problematic.

2. Look up two of the signers of the Declaration of Independence and note something interesting about each of them. Where did they live? When were they born? What did they believe?

3. Activity: The Ultimate Break-Up Letter (Colonies to England)

   Handwrite the following letter:

   I'm not sure how to start this letter, but I feel we need to talk. I've been thinking about us a lot lately. I really thought we'd be together forever, but things have changed. I feel that you have taken me for granted. You just started doing whatever you wanted and never asked me how I felt about it. I have been thinking about this a lot lately, and I don't want to hurt you. But I think it's time we broke up.

Signed,

The 13 Colonies

Tell your audience that you found this letter written by your child or one of the school children in the office, etc. This is an attention grabber.

Read the body of the letter. However, pause before you read who signed the letter ("The 13 Colonies"). Ask your audience member about their thoughts as to who might have written the letter. Undoubtedly, there will be laughter and maybe some uneasiness.

Tell the audience that this is the ultimate breakup letter by the thirteen colonies from Britain.

Discuss the reasons for the breakup.

Discuss the principles relied upon by Thomas Jefferson to justify separation, namely the right of revolution, natural rights, and popular sovereignty.

Discussion Questions

1. What is the philosophy of government set forth in the Declaration of Independence and how does this philosophy shape our current governmental system?

2. Upon what creed was the U.S. government founded?

3. What is the purpose of government?

4. What is the right of revolution referred to in the Declaration of Independence?

5. What provisions do you appreciate the most about the Declaration of Independence?

Chapter 5
Brave Men Rise Up:
Feeling What the Founders Felt

"If Historiographers should be hardy enough to fill the page of History with the advantages that have been gained with unequal numbers, on the part of America, in the course of this contest, and attempt to relate the distressing circumstances under which they have been obtained, it is more than probable that Posterity will bestow on their labors the epithet and marks of fiction; for it will not be believed that such a force as Great Britain has employed for eight years in this Country could be baffled in their plan of Subjugating it by numbers infinitely less, composed of Men oftentimes half starved; always in Rags, without pay, and experiencing, at times, every species of distress which human nature is capable of undergoing."

~George Washington
Letter to Major General Nathaniel Greene, February 6, 1783

As the British engaged in war with the colonies, they had many advantages, including a large, well-trained army and navy, with many Loyalists in the colonies who supported the British Empire. However, many of those colonists were alienated by Lord Dunmore's promise of freedom to slaves who joined the British army and resisted offering support to anyone other than the Loyalists. On the other hand, many colonists were inspired by Thomas Paine's pamphlet, "Common Sense," which was the clarion call to preserve what rightfully belongs to every human being, namely freedom. Large opposing factions were created at the outset of this conflict that rested on short-term and long-term motives, such as property and method of governance.

Ulimately, a combination of excellent leadership by George Washington, aid from European nations such as France, and tactical errors committed by British commanders contributed to an American victory. The initial British strategy called for crushing the rebellion in the north, and, on several occasions, the British nearly defeated the Continental Army. However, victories at Trenton and Princeton, N.J., in late 1776 and early 1777 restored the patriots' hopes. Then, a victory at Saratoga, N.Y., halted the British advance from Canada, and led to France's intervention on behalf of the patriot rebels.

On December 25, 1776, George Washington and his troops were literally on the brink of disaster. His army had been whittled down from 25,000 to a mere 2,500. Yes, only one in 10 remained with the courage to fight with General Washington on Christmas Day 1776. And of those 2,500, one-third had no shoes. Many literally had to wrap their feet in burlap to deal with the frigid and icy conditions. Up to that point, they had engaged in numerous battles, retreated rapidly, and lost many troops along the way.

As Washington contemplated the dire circumstances on the shores of the Delaware River, he wrote "Victory or Death" on small pieces of paper—the watchword for the attack. On that day, the battle-ravaged patriots crossed the icy Delaware River, marched to Trenton, and defeated and captured 700 professional Hessian soldiers. The courageous victory revitalized the legitimacy of the revolution.

Shortly after this victory, all of the enlistments for the entire army were up. On December 31, 1776, George Washington addressed his troops, knowing they were free to go the following day. He called on his troops to reenlist, but no one stepped forward even though Washington offered significant incentives to stay. Washington left on horseback and returned a short time later and addressed them once again.

"My brave fellows, you have done all I asked you to do, and more than can be reasonably expected; but your country is at stake, your wives, your houses and all that you hold dear. You have worn yourselves out with

fatigues and hardships, but we know not how to spare you. If you will consent to stay one month longer, you will render that service to the cause of liberty, and to your country, which you probably can never do under any other circumstances."

After this short plea, the men began stepping forward. This monumental event is largely an unspoken and unknown victory of the American revolution, namely ensuring that the battle could continue on with an adequate army in place.

In the Winter of 1777 and the Spring of 1778, Washington set up an encampment at Valley Forge. Plagued with bad weather and poor conditions, it would prove a critical turning point for the Continental Army. Training, equipment, and supplies would improve, and the soldiers brought a renewed spirit to the fight for independence.

In 1778, the fighting shifted to the south. Britain's forces succeeded in capturing Georgia and Charleston, S.C. and defeating the American army at Camden, S.C., but bands of patriots harassed the loyalists and disrupted British supply lines. Significantly, however, the powerful British forces were unable to achieve control over the southern countryside before advancing northward to Virginia. Then, in 1781, an American and French force defeated the British at Yorktown in the war's last major battle.

Many battles occurred throughout the Revolutionary War, and you are encouraged to study them. However, at a minimum you should understand the great sacrifice of those men and women who fought for American freedom. The battles ensued for many years and finally ceased in 1783. The finality of the war was memorialized in 1784 in the Treaty of Paris.

Over 230 battles took place over a six-year period, which included naval and offshore raids and skirmishes. Below are some of the more significant battles. See Appendix D for a more comprehensive list of the battles that took place, along with a list of casualties.

4/19/1775	The Battles of Lexington and Concord . . . . Lexington and Concord Massachusetts
5/10/1775	The Siege of Fort Ticonderoga . . Fort Ticonderoga, New York
5/27/1775	The Battle of Chelsea Creek . . . Suffolk County, Massachusetts
6/16/1775	The Battle of Bunker (Breeds) Hill . . . . Charlestown, Massachusetts
12/31/1775	The Battle of Quebec . . . . . . Quebec City, Province of Quebec
8/27/1776	The Battle of Long Island (Brooklyn Heights) . . . . Long Island, New York
10/28/1776	The Battle of White Plains . . . . White Plains, New York
11/16/1776	The Battle of Fort Washington . . . . . Washington Heights, Manhattan, New York
12/26/1776	The Battle of Trenton . . . . Trenton, New Jersey
1/3/1777	The Battle of Princeton . . . . Princeton, New Jersey
8/6/1777	The Battle of Oriskany . . . . Oriskany, New York
8/16/1777	The Battle of Bennington . . . . Bennington, New York
9/11/1777	The Battle of Brandywine . . . Near Chadds Ford, Pennsylvania
9/19/1777	The Battle of Saratoga (Freeman's Farm) . . . . Saratoga County, New York
10/4/1777	The Battle of Germantown . . . . . . Germantown, Pennsylvania
10/7/1777	The Battle of Saratoga (Bemis Heights) . . . . Saratoga County, New York
6/28/1778	The Battle of Monmouth . . . . Monmouth, New Jersey
12/29/1778	The Capture of Savannah . . . . Savannah, Georgia
3/29/1780	The Siege of Charleston . . . . Charleston, South Carolina
8/16/1780	The Battle of Camden . . . . . North of Camden, South Carolina
10/7/1780	The Battle of King's Mountain . . . . . Near Blackburn, SC and King's Mountain, NC
1/17/1781	The Battle of Cowpens . . . . Cowpens, South Carolina

3/15/1781	The Battle of Guilford Courthouse . . . . Guilford Courthouse, North Carolina
9/8/1781	The Battle of Eutaw Springs . . . . Near present-day Eutawville, South Carolina
10/9/1781	The Battle of Yorktown . . . . Yorktown, Virginia

What were the ultimate consequences of the Revolutionary War?

1. About 7,200 Americans died in battle during the Revolution. Another 10,000 died from disease or exposure and about 8,500 died in British prisons.

2. The states began adopting written constitutions that guaranteed their unalienable rights and began to more firmly establish their government. Just as important, they began to act as independent states.

3. England lost her colonies in America, and England's national debt increased to a great extent. The British were learning how to manage their newly-earned "super power" status as a result of the previously-fought French-Indian War.

4. The colonists gave birth to a new nation. The founders literally pledged everything, and they accomplished something that would be embraced as the "Great American Experiment." This experiment would be looked to for generations to come. More importantly, however, the actions of those brave men and women would be revered as action that was essential to begin a revolution for liberty, not just in America but throughout the world.

Lesson

1. Debate: Many accuse the founders of working to establish a system that would make them wealthy. Some claim that they were only concerned about their property, their money, and their future. Others claim that they were truly fighting for a more noble, unselfish cause that hinged on freedom for all. What are the arguments for

and against each position? As you make these arguments, think of examples in your life where you have done things for selfish purposes and other things out of more pure motives. What was the underlying motivations behind these actions that can be compared to the founders?

2. Tell the story of December 25, 1776 in a way that will captivate your audience and set a somber mood. They will experience just a hint of what George Washington and the patriots who fought and died for our freedom went through.

> Gather your group around a swimming pool, lake, ocean, or any body of water. To have the greatest impact, this lesson should be taught when it is cold outside. You should call everyone together and discuss some of your thoughts about the warriors who fought for freedom. Engage your audience by having them talk about some of the great moments of the Revolutionary War. You will then tell the story of General Washington and the crossing of the Delaware. As you begin to talk about the harsh weather conditions and the fact that so few were actually prepared for the tough winter conditions, you should enter the water to at least waist level with all of your clothes on. No swimsuits allowed, as this stunt is not for the weak! Continue telling the story and encourage others to enter along with you. This moving and powerful lesson will create a memory of a lifetime and allow one to experience just a hint of what it must have felt like to be George Washington or one of his troops. Consider creating a tradition of commemorating the "Crossing of the Delaware" every Christmas day.

> For the modified version, get a bucket of ice and allow others to place their feet or hands inside the bucket. As they do so, tell the story of Washington crossing the Delaware River.

Discussion Questions

1. Who is your favorite founding father and why?

2. What does it mean to be courageous? Why must one be courageous in order to protect freedom?

3. Research one of the battles fought during the Revolutionary War and discuss the details.

4. Why did the Continental Army agree to fight against the most powerful military in the world? What was their philosophy and do you agree?

5. How do you think George Washington must have felt as he faced numerous defeats yet knew he was fighting for a cause that would impact his countrymen and the cause of freedom?

6. Were the founders justified in going to war? Why or why not?

7. A good percentage of the population were apathetic to the cause of the patriot rebels. What does it ultimately take to mobilize the mainstream to a cause that is relatively unpopular?

Chapter 6
Rights v. Privileges

"The jaws of power are always open to devour, and her arm is always stretched out, if possible, to destroy the freedom of thinking, speaking, and writing."
~John Adams

In order to understand liberty, one must understand the distinction between rights and privileges. Beyond understanding what rights are, one must understand the distinction between inalienable rights and vested (civil) rights.

As a general rule, a "right" is power inherent in one person and bestowed on an individual by the Creator or by virtue of one's humanity. Stated differently, a right encompasses the sovereign authority to do (or not do) something because there is no higher authority from whom one must obtain permission to act. In other words, no government, king, or individual gives us rights. We are born with them.

As a reminder of what we discussed in Chapter One, we have the inherent right to think what we wish, say what we think, and write what we say. Those things that we generate through our own productivity are ours to keep and have stewardship over. We have the natural right to protect and defend ourselves and have the right to be left alone in and on our own property. The government's purpose is to recognize, acknowledge, and protect these various rights.

A privilege, on the other hand, is something that requires temporary permission granted by someone in authority. For example, if a non-citizen were to come to the United States to work, the government could issue a visa granting the privilege to work in this country. In addition, if the government grants a company a contract to build a new government facility, that is a privilege as well.

Now, let's go back to "rights," as opposed to "privileges." We must recognize that almost all rights hinge on the existence of property rights. The right of life and liberty exist and are protected so long as the right of property is protected. John Adams said that "[t]he moment the idea is admitted into society that property is not as sacred as the laws of God, and that there is not a force of law and public justice to protect it, anarchy and tyranny commence. If 'Thou shalt not covet' and `Thou shalt not steal' were not commandments of Heaven, they must be made inviolable precepts in every society before it can be civilized or made free."

Let's look at a few examples illustrating how our liberties are inextricably intertwined with property rights. Do you have the fundamental right to speak? Absolutely. However, can you go into your neighbor's house and say whatever you wish without any concern that you may be removed from the home? Or what about going into someone else's private business and picketing inside the store itself? You likely would not be allowed, and generally would not have the "right," to do either because your right to speak hinges on property that you own or, as a taxpayer, contribute to building and maintaining (e.g., public sidewalks, etc.). If the property does not belong to you, your liberties may be significantly diminished, if not non-existent.

Another way of understanding this principle is to recognize that the only limitation on your rights (in this case, speech) is the rights of others (property). For example, your freedom or right to swing your fist stops at your neighbor's chin.

It is also important to understand some of the differences that revolve around the nature of various fundamental rights. Fundamental rights fit within two categories, namely unalienable rights and vested rights. An unalienable right is endowed by the Creator or is inherent in each person simply by virtue of their humanity. A vested or civil right typically is a legally-protected quasi-right designed to protect unalienable rights from being infringed upon by others or the government.

Later on we'll discuss the details of the Constitution, but let's take a glimpse at the Bill of Rights for just a moment to identify some of the various rights secured through the document. What is critical to understand is that the founders recognized the distinction and solidified their understanding in our ruling document.

Unalienable Rights   Vested Rights

Unalienable Rights	Vested Rights
Life (5th and 14th Amendments)	Fair Trial (6th Amendment)
Acquire, possess, and enjoy property	Public Trial (6th Amendment)
Speech (1st Amendment)	Speedy Trial (6th Amendment)
Assembly (1st Amendment)	Right to confront accuser (6th Amendment)
Press (1st Amendment)	Right to hear allegations made by the government (6th Amendment)
Self Defense (2nd Amendment)	Right to counsel (6th Amendment)
Marriage	Right to have case heard in the jurisdiction where the alleged crime occurred (6thAmendment)
Right to be left alone (4th Amendment)	Right to avoid being forced to speak to help build the government's case (5th Amendment)
Procreation	Presumption of innocence; Burden of proof remains with the government (5th Amendment)
Pursuit of things of interest to you (job, education, etc.)	Right to ensure the government has a warrant before seizing or searching your property (4th Amendment)

You will notice that all of the rights listed in the left column are rights that a person is born with, i.e., they are inherent in every human being. The rights listed in the right column were put in place by our framers to ensure maximum protection of our unalienable rights, such as those in the left column, from government infringement or intrusion.

As you have read up to this point, you may wonder why it is necessary to outline the unalienable rights of human beings in our Constitution, specifically our Bill of Rights, if they are, in fact, inherent in every being. Is it necessary that some of our unalienable rights are enumerated in the Constitution? The answer is a resounding "Yes!"

While the Constitution doesn't give us any unalienable rights, it does put government on notice as to its obligation to protect the people's unalienable rights. Remember that it is the primary obligation of government to secure the rights of the people. Moreover, while not every unalienable right is listed in the Constitution, such rights don't cease to exist simply because they are not enumerated. The framers simply included some of the more important rights and then made it clear in the Ninth Amendment that the enumeration of rights did not mean that other unenumerated rights "retained by the people" could be denied or disparaged.

John Dickinson said, "Kings or parliaments could not give the rights essential to happiness....We claim them from a higher source....They are born with us; exist with us; and cannot be taken from us by any human power, without taking our lives." In other words, we must defend our liberties from infringement, and defend our Constitution from being assaulted. Freedom depends on it.

Lesson

1. Make a list like the one outlined above. On the left column, write "Unalienable Rights" and, on the right column, write "Vested Rights." You will then lead a discussion differentiating between the two. Remember, unalienable

rights are those inherent in every human being. Vested rights are those put in place to protect unalienable rights from being infringed upon. The government may, in fact, infringe on liberty to some degree so long as due process (the vested right to fundamental fairness) is satisfied. We do so with criminals every day. However, before liberty can be deprived, vested rights must be honored.

2. This fun exercise and object lesson will require the planning with at least one other person who will act as a "plant." To really have an impact, plan to lead the discussion at someone else's home. Tell the homeowner that during the lesson you will go into the person's refrigerator, pantry, etc. and just help yourself to food, drink, etc. For emphasis, do not laugh, joke, or make light of the situation. Simply begin enjoying the food. Someone will certainly ask what you are doing, and you will respond by saying, "What do you mean? I have the fundamental right to eat?" This is a great illustration of how a person's unalienable rights hinge on property rights. Of course, you have the right to eat. However, you do not have the right to eat something that doesn't belong to you. Have fun using variations of this object lesson. It is a rather powerful illustration.

Discussion Questions

1. What is a right? How is a right different from a privilege?

2. Where do our rights come from? How do you know this?

3. Can a right ever be taken away? Under what circumstances?

4. What is the difference between an unalienable right and a vested right? Give examples.

5. Discuss and give examples of how our unalienable rights revolve around our property rights.

Chapter 7
Philosophy of American Government

"A free people [claim] their rights as derived from the laws of nature, and not as the gift of their chief magistrate."
~Thomas Jefferson

The philosophy of American government is to acknowledge and protect the inherent liberties of the people. As solidified in the Declaration of Independence, it is this very philosophy that makes America unique in more ways than one.

The Declaration of Independence is the "why" and the Constitution is the "how." The Declaration of Independence is the "promise." The Constitution is the "fulfillment." The Declaration of Independence is what our early founders were willing to die for. The Constitution is what they were willing to live for.

The Declaration of Independence outlines rather forcefully the nature of man and the fact that man is, indeed, born to be free. It was necessary for America to powerfully and succinctly articulate the justification for their independence. And Thomas Jefferson did so remarkably well. In the second paragraph of the Declaration of Independence, Jefferson hits on the very philosophy of government upon which America would be grounded.

"We hold these truths to be self-evident, that all men are created equal, that they are endowed by their Creator with certain unalienable Rights, that among these are Life, Liberty and the pursuit of Happiness."

Thomas Jefferson made several important points that deserve attention.

1. "We hold these truths….": The founders were not postulating mere opinions, ideas, thoughts, or contemplations.

They were dealing with what they believed were irrefutable, undeniable truths.

2. "....to be self-evident....": The founders did not believe those truths were debatable. In other words, they were self-evident. The alternative is to believe that man was born to be a subject and slave to others. Notably, Thomas Jefferson initially wrote, "We hold these truths to be sacred and undeniable." Benjamin Franklin replaced the words "sacred and undeniable" with the term "self-evident." Either way, they believed that the inherent freedom of human beings could not be ignored, redefined, or negotiated.

3. "....that all men are created equal....": The founders believed in the ideal that all men are of equal moral worth and are born equal under the law. No man has a right to govern others without their consent. Consequently, people have the right to pursue their interests, their passions, and their heart's desires without direction, interference, or help from others. Essentially, human beings are sovereign and independent, and government should not dictate the course that one's life should take or attempt to ensure equality of outcome. Government should only, at most, ensure equal treatment under the law. Indeed, equality is found in liberty and not in restraint and servitude.

4. "....that they are endowed by their Creator with certain unalienable rights....": Unalienable rights do not come from other men, government, laws, or even written constitutions. They come from our Creator and exist simply by virtue of our humanity. Our founders understood that the moment we believe that our rights come from other individuals or government, this is the moment that we relinquish our freedom to others.

5. "....that among these are life, liberty, and the pursuit of happiness.": Every human being has the right to life, liberty, and the pursuit of happiness. The words "that among

these...." simply mean that the framers were not creating an all-encompassing list, only a list that was broad enough to convey some of the more important liberties and the idea that those rights come from something or somebody other than ourselves.

The Declaration of Independence is the greatest declaration of human rights penned by man. It is imperative that those who understand and defend America understand this very basic philosophy of our government, for if one changes the philosophy of the "why," namely the Declaration of Independence, one can easily change the "how," namely our Constitution.

Lesson

1. Evaluate the influence that the Declaration of Independence has had on the rest of the world. What other movements have utilized the principles of the Declaration of Independence to mobilize the people? A few examples include the "French Declaration of Rights of Man" and the "Declaration of Sentiments" proposed at the Seneca Falls Convention. Did those movements rely on a sound philosophy that would constitute good government? For further support, review John Locke's writings about the fundamental nature of man.

2. Group Activity and Illustration. Bring your group together and designate yourself as the leader. Explain to your audience that you are going to establish the rules of a society that everyone is going to be a part of. Utilizing the philosophy of Plato and Thomas Hobbes, explain that people are generally inclined towards greed and power and, as a result, tend to hurt one another. Therefore, you will ensure that such inclinations are not carried out. You will dictate where each person lives, how they will contribute to society, and assist in accommodating any needs they may have. Have fun and even talk specifically about the duties of the group members. After doing so, talk

about the advantages and disadvantages of this philosophy. Ultimately, you want to illustrate that this form of government is not consistent with the philosophy of government established in the Declaration of Independence.

3. Debate: An individual shows up in your community and decides to burn the American flag, which you find despicable. What is the proper function of government under these circumstances?

Discussion Questions

1. Describe in your own words the philosophy of good government.

2. Is the statement "our rights are derived from a creator" a self-evident truth? What are the political and social consequences of adhering to or disregarding this idea?

3. Why is it important to recognize the roots of our rights and what would happen if that philosophy were altered?

4. What does it mean to say that we are created equal? Equality of outcome? Equality of opportunity? Equality under the law?

5. Give examples of liberty and the pursuit of happiness as mentioned in the Declaration of Independence.

6. Is there a difference between the "pursuit of happiness" and the "right to be happy"? What is the difference?

7. The Declaration of Independence notes the right of life, liberty, and the pursuit of happiness. Is this list all encompassing or simply a reflection of the overarching idea of freedom? Is it possible to create an exhaustive list of all of the liberties one could possibly enjoy? Explain.

Chapter 8
Purpose of Government

"Government...should be formed to secure and enlarge the exercise of the natural rights of its members; and every government which has not this in view as its principal object is not a government of a legitimate kind."
~James Wilson

The power and authority to establish a government begins with the people. In turn, government has a very specific responsibility, and that responsibility is first and foremost to protect the rights of the people. Thomas Jefferson noted in the Declaration of Independence that "[t]o secure these rights [life, liberty, and the pursuit of happiness], governments are instituted among men."

Even though government has the duty to protect our inherent liberties, governments historically have intruded on individual rights to establish more control over the people or, ostensibly, to ensure public safety. Americans must be vigilant not to fall into the trap of believing that public safety or the desires of the people in power are more important that individual liberty and freedom. Freedom always comes with some risk.

Consider the following: A person has the fundamental right to defend himself. One day, an enraged man goes on a shooting spree. How do we resolve this tragedy? Do we pass laws that it make it more difficult for law-abiding citizens to obtain firearms, knowing full well that criminals will access them regardless of the law, or do we foster an environment of encouraging people to learn to defend themselves? The former solution leads to tyranny and a more dangerous society. The latter embraces a free society populated by responsible citizens. If a people wish to remove the potential of the risk that comes with freedom, they will find themselves living as subjects or, even worse, slaves.

As George Washington stated, "Government is not reason; it is not eloquent; it is force. Like fire, it is a dangerous servant and a fearful master." We, the people, are the masters of government and must ensure that those in power live up to their duty. As we do so, we must be vigilant to ensure that the laws created by the government revolve around protecting the rights of the people.

There is a rather easy formula that will help determine whether a law is legitimate or not based upon two irreducible principles. Anytime you are confronted by some proposed government action, consider the following and ask yourself whether the action falls within the scope of protecting the rights of individual citizens. If government action falls outside of these two areas, the proposed policy, law, or regulation should be deemed suspect.

1. Don't infringe on the rights of others; and

2. Keep your word.

"Don't infringe on the rights of others" is the basis for all criminal and tort law. Stated differently, murder, burglary, rape, and robbery are all punishable by law because they infringe on the rights of others. However, we wouldn't punish someone for standing on their head, scratching their ear, or running with scissors because the rights of others are not infringed upon through these actions.

"Keep your word" is the basis of all contract law. If two parties engage in a contract and there is a breach or violation of the contract, the law should provide a remedy. Again, these are legitimate laws and an appropriate function of government.

As people subject themselves to the control of government, it is critical that there is a clear understanding as to the scope of government's job and power. It is not government's role to take care of the few at the majority's expense; nor is it to take care of the majority at the minority's expense. It is to protect our freedom to make choices without government policies and regulations or other people infringing on, or otherwise interfering with, that freedom. The scope of government action should be simply to ensure that rights are protected and that our ability to choose is ultimately maximized.

Lesson

1. Write two columns on a board or piece of paper. On the top of one column write "Good Law," and on the other column write "Bad Law." You then want to bring up several examples to discuss and have the group determine if the law is legitimate or not. The measuring stick will be whether the law protects society from having someone infringe on individual rights or not keeping their word. See below for a few examples.

   a. Murder—Good law because the act of taking another life infringes on the fundamental right of life of another.

   b. Theft—Good law because the act of taking the property of another infringes on the fundamental right of another to possess and retain his own property.

   c. Law that provides for a remedy when someone doesn't keep their contractual agreement—Good law because one may not give their word, bargain for something of value, and not keep their end of the deal.

   d. Law forbidding one from running with scissors—Bad law because the action of an individual running with scissors does not infringe on the rights of others.

   e. Law mandating the taking of someone's money in order to take care of the poor—Bad law because it infringes on the property rights of another. Welfare is not the job of the government but the job of individuals and charitable groups.

    f. Law forbidding protesting on a street corner in a downtown metropolitan area—Bad law because it infringes on the individual's right of free speech.

2. Debate what government should do under certain circumstances. Example: An individual is burning the American flag or the Holy Bible on public property. The people in the area are offended and become disruptive themselves. Some even become violent. If you were a police officer, whose primary job is to protect the rights of the people, what would you do? Would you stop the actions of those burning the flag or the Bibles, thereby preserving public safety, or would you stop the angry crowd, thereby preserving speech and expression? Remember that the default position in America should be liberty with a few exceptions. Do these examples fit within the exception?

Discussion Questions

1. Is government necessary? Why or why not?

2. What is the purpose of government?

3. What are the advantages and disadvantages of government? How can we measure whether government is operating within its proper parameters of ensuring that the liberties of the people are protected?

4. What are some examples of ways in which government exceeds its purpose?

5. What can be done when government expands beyond their fundamental purpose?

6. Should government play a different role at the federal level as compared to the state level regarding the protection of liberty? Explain.

Chapter 9
Popular Sovereignty: The People Speak

"Liberty at all hazards must be supported."
~John Adams

The Declaration of Independence reminds us that the purpose of government is to secure and protect the rights of the people. However, where does the government get the authority to do this? Is it determined by the most powerful who use force to assume the role of a dictator? Is it determined by a man who claims God told him to step in as an authority figure, namely a theocracy? Is it determined by family lineage, as seen in an aristocracy? The answer is none of the above.

The Declaration of Independence tells us that the power to govern is derived from the "consent of the governed." In other words, the people are sovereign, govern themselves, and should determine who their leaders are. Popular sovereignty represents the idea that the ultimate power to govern resides within each individual. What is important to note here is the while people have the power to govern themselves, they do not have the power to trample on the rights of other human beings.

No man has the authority to exercise unfettered power and to dictate how human beings will live their lives without those people giving consent through the election process and the ratification of a ruling document. Political authority flows from the people, and government can exercise only that authority given by the people. That argument was the essence of the American revolution and was the impetus for, and the backbone of, the Declaration of Independence.

Popular sovereignty is a fundamental component of a republican form of government. A republic is designed to protect all people. However, a republic can only truly work if the people are educated, vigilant, and active in the process. If the governed become lazy or apathetic, history tells us that tyranny and absolute rule are on the horizon.

As you begin to understand how profound the concept of popular sovereignty is, you will begin to understand how different America is. Consider the revolutions that have been fought throughout history. What was the result of those revolutions? Let's take a look.

What did Russia get as a result of its revolution? Stalin. How about France? Napoleon. What about China? Mao. What did America get? It didn't get any particular individual. Further, they would not kill each other as a general rule, as is so typical in so many revolutions. Instead, they would argue with each other. They would engage and dialogue with one another. They would consult with one another for the cause of liberty. Indeed, like so many other revolutions throughout history, ours was a process of changing the political structure and not necessarily the social structure.

Our founders agreed on a few things, namely the fundamental nature of man and how power corrupts and changes people and the fact that man is born to be free. While they agreed on those two very important principles, they disagreed at times as to how to limit government and protect the rights of the people. In other words, they recognized the profound principle of power in the people (i.e., popular sovereignty) and were on a mission to determine how to best structure a government system that would minimize the possibility of tyranny and maximize individual liberties.

Today we must be united on a common foundation and ensure that liberty prevails. Of course, we may disagree as to the execution of certain ideas. However, it is through the marketplace of ideas that we insure that freedom's torch is passed on from one generation to the next.

Lesson

1. Debate: Imagine that you live in a community of 1000 people. Of the 1000 citizens, 999 are Catholics and the remaining one person is a Buddhist. Should the 999 be able to show up at the ballot box and determine what religion may or may not be practiced in the community? As you respond, discuss the difference between deciding on a system of governance and what people may legitimately decide upon through this process. Even though people have the right to decide upon their form of government, should that ever include restricting the liberties of the people through a majority vote?

2. Debate: To what degree should the people have a voice?

   We vote in our leaders. However, should our leaders always follow the "voice of the people"? What if you had 100 people in a community and 99 of them were opposed to eating broccoli? Should that 99, through the actions of their elected representatives, be able to take the right of the one? What if it does not involve the eating of broccoli but instead involves smoking marijuana, viewing pornography, or marrying someone of the same sex?

   Remember that the power to govern begins with the people. A republican form of government ensures that rights are protected regardless of what the majority may say. How do we best ensure that we have an actively-engaged citizenry but that they do not find ways to trump the rights of others with whom they disagree? Consider the question again after reviewing Chapter 10.

3. Divide your group into two teams.

   Question: Should voter ballot initiatives be allowed to overturn laws passed by legislative bodies? Stated differently, should the people be able to overturn the actions of their legislators through the ballot box?

49

a. Team A: Yes. Ballot initiatives allow voters to directly participate in their government, as this reflects power in the people to ultimately govern.

b. Team B: No. Voters already express their views through the election of public officials and voter initiatives defy a republican form of government.

Discussion Questions

1. What is popular sovereignty and why is it considered a fundamental part of a republican form of government?

2. What is the relationship between popular sovereignty, limited government, and citizenship?

3. Are there limitations on the voice of the people and what they should be able to vote on? If so, what are those limitations?

4. Why are a vigilant people necessary in a governmental system that revolves around protecting the liberty of the people and not necessarily the power of those whom we elect?

5. What responsibilities should citizens fulfill in order for a republican form of government to succeed?

6. Can the majority of the people give away their right and authority to govern and elect to have a dictator rule over them? What about the minority who do not wish to submit to a dictatorial form of government?

Chapter 10

Different Forms of Government: Why a Republican Form of Government is Superior

"A republic if you can keep it."
~Benjamin Franklin

Article IV of the U.S. Constitution guarantees every state a republican form of government, which is truly a form of government that every American should cherish and nurture. Many forms of government have existed throughout history. Let's take a look at some of them and what they consist of. We will discover why a republican form of government, if adopted and protected, is the most advantageous to a society that wishes to be free.

1. Monarchy—This is a system of government where one person has all of the power. It is generally in the form of a king or dictator. The problem is that there are not checks and balances on the king and, therefore, he can rule without being accountable to the people or to any other branch of government.

2. Oligarchy—In reality, true monarchies never really exist. Monarchies are more often than not oligarchies. An oligarchy is the rule by a few with one or two men at the forefront as the leaders. This is a very common form of government.

3. Anarchy—This theoretical form of government means no government rule at all. If anarchy ever existed, its life has been short lived because it is generally a group that will rise up to stop the lack of rule. Yes, the very people who start revolutions and advocate anarchy are almost always the people who rise up, stop the disorder, and take charge. Anarchy is a lie, almost always evolves into an oli-

garchy, and is an impossible way to live. History teaches us this lesson all too well.

4. Democracy—This is a system of government that is run by the majority of people. Like an oligarchy or monarchy, it is a poor system of government. Nowhere in the Declaration of Independence or the U.S. Constitution will one find the word "democracy." In fact, the very word evoked negative passions and emotions early on in our history. Thomas Jefferson referenced the "tyranny of the majority." Elbridge Gerry, a delegate from Massachusetts, warned of the "excesses of democracy." Alexander Hamilton of New York claimed that the people "seldom judge or determine right." Edmund Randolph, a delegate and the governor of Virginia, pleaded for a form of government that would "restrain the fury of democracy." Finally, when William Paterson of New Jersey noted that the "democratic spirit beats high" at the time of the Convention of 1787, it was most certainly meant to be a derisive attack on the lack of wisdom demonstrated by the people. Scottish historian Alexander Tytler perhaps said it best.

> "A democracy is always temporary in nature; it simply cannot exist as a permanent form of government. A democracy will continue to exist up until the time that voters discover that they can vote themselves generous gifts from the public treasury. From that moment on, the majority always votes for the candidates who promise the most benefits from the public treasury, with the result that every democracy will finally collapse due to loose fiscal policy, which is always followed by a dictatorship. The average age of the world's greatest civilizations from the beginning of history has been about 200 years."

5. Republic—A republican form of government embraces the rule of law. As previously noted, Article IV of the United States Constitution guarantees that every state

shall have a republican form of government. The Pledge of Allegiance talks about a republic, and, of course, our founders talked repeatedly of our constitutional republic. A republican form of government guarantees the fundamental liberties of the people regardless of whether a person exercising a particular right does not sit well with the majority. The government has an obligation to protect the rights of all of the people. A republic is to a democracy what gold is to trash. The gold must be protected, and the trash, i.e., the danger of a democracy, must be tossed to the wayside.

There are many forms of government, and the list in this chapter is not exhaustive. However, most governments can really be narrowed down to one of two alternatives: Oligarchy or a republic.

True democracies never last long, as they evolve into a scheme where a few in power are making the rules. A monarchy is rare as well. Very seldom has one man successfully led a society. It may appear as though one individual man is leading, but, without question, there is almost always a group of individuals leading and providing direction behind the scenes. Anarchies have never sustained themselves, as the most powerful within the culture will ultimately rise up and control.

So, we are left with few choices: An oligarchy or a republic. Which will we choose?

Lesson

1. Debate—Divide into two groups and debate the following question: What should be the role of citizens in creating laws and policies? (Consider what should happen if the majority wanted to get rid of all McDonald's restaurants. Is this permissible?) As we debated in Chapter 9, this discussion may once again evolve into one about initiatives, referendums, and recall elections.

a. Team A: Public policy and the laws should reflect the opinion of the voters

b. Team B: Public policy and the laws should be created by officials who are most informed about the issues and who have taken an oath to uphold the Constitution.

2. Billy Steals Your Horse—Have fun with this one! Take one person from your group and bring him to the front of the room. Tell everyone that you, the ranch owner, saw this person riding away on your horse. You tell the townspeople to pursue the alleged thief, and they bring him back to town. You make your plea to the residents and ask, "All those in favor of hanging this man, raise your hand." A majority vote would result in the participant's death regardless of whether a crime was actually proven. The whims of democracy are dangerous.

Now, outline the same scenario and upon asking, "All those in favor of hanging this man?," explain that the Sheriff arrives (which can be one of your participants). The Sheriff is a member of the executive branch of government that enforces the law but also ensures that the rights of all people are protected. In this case, the people are trying to infringe on this person's liberty interests short of due process. In turn, the Sheriff says: "You can't hang this man. He has rights. He has the right to a fair trial, a public trial, and a speedy trial. He has the right to the presumption of innocence and to have the government prove its case beyond a reasonable doubt. He has a right to hear the allegations being made against him and to confront his accusers. He has a right to remain silent, and he has a right to an impartial jury. And none of you buckaroos appear to very impartial. No, you can't hang this man!" After going through this presentation, take a look at the Fifth and Sixth Amendments, and you will see the enumeration of these liberties outlined in the response by the Sheriff. This presentation is an example of a republican form of government.

Discussion Questions

1. What is a republican form of government and how does it differ from a democracy?

2. What are the advantages and disadvantages of living in a republican form of government?

3. What are the differences between a monarchy, an oligarchy, a democracy, and anarchy? How do these forms of government compare to a republican form of government?

4. In what ways has America distanced itself from a constitutional republic? In what ways are the principles of a constitutional republic firmly in tact?

5. How would you respond to a claim that a democracy and a republic are the same thing? What is the response to the claim that we need to "spread democracy throughout the world"?

Chapter 11
America's First Constitution:
Articles of Confederation

"The advice nearest to my heart and deepest in my
convictions is that the union of the states
be cherished and perpetuated."
~James Madison

After 56 men signed the Declaration of Independence, America recognized that a constitution was desperately needed to establish the rule of law and to avoid experiencing the problems from which they had just escaped. Our founders recognized the importance of outlining the parameters for government power. Because those men had just experienced tyranny, they sought to set up a government that maximized freedom and limited government power. While they knew government was necessary, they also knew what a runaway, limitless government was capable of.

In 1777, the Articles of Confederation were proposed and adopted, and it was ratified in 1781. Under the Articles, the "federal" government had several powers:

1. Power to petition the states for money

2. To make and wage war

3. Appoint ambassadors

4. To enter into treaties

5. Appoint officers to the military

6. Establish maritime courts

7. Authority to settle border disputes between states

8. Regulate trade with Indian tribes

9. Set up post offices and charge postage

However, as good of an effort as the initial effort was, there were glaring omissions that caused problems throughout the country. Some of those concerns were as follows:

1. Only one branch of government existed, namely the legis-lature. There was no executive or judicial branch. As a re-sult, the ability to enforce federal law or have a court interpret the propriety of federal action or to simply act as a check was virtually non-existent.

2. Congress had no means of enforcing its decrees. There-fore, whether the states complied with the decrees or laws enacted by the legislature were dependent solely on the whims of the respective states. For example, if mili-tary action was deemed necessary, Congress could only hope that the states would agree to provide the funds to pay for such action. That rarely occurred.

3. Any time Congress was to vote on an issue, each state had one vote. As a result, smaller states had more power than the larger states. States like Rhode Island (also known as "Rogue Island") rarely voted to do anything that would re-quire federal action. As a result, virtually nothing was ever accomplished.

4. The states acted as independent sovereigns. For example, individual states negotiated treaties with foreign countries without regard to the surrounding states.

5. Congress had no power to regulate commercial activity among the states. As a result, the states engaged in trade wars. For example, if New York had a contract with a ship-ping company to bring in goods, Georgia would have to spend additional and often exorbitant amounts of money to have those goods shipped to the state. Why? Because as the goods moved from state to state, additional tariffs and taxes were imposed. As a result, the states were at odds.

6. Congress had no power to tax, and, of course, every gov-ernment needs money in order to function. Congress sent out requisitions to the various states to collect money, but

the states rarely complied, which quickly created a financial disaster for the federal government.

7. It was extremely difficult to get anything done given the level of state participation required under the Articles of Confederation. For example, a unanimous vote of the states was required to amend the Articles, and two-thirds of the states had to consent to enact proposed legislation. Predictably, virtually nothing could be accomplished under that system.

As 1787 approached, a mere six years into the national experiment, the treasury was empty, the states were paralyzed with debt, the people were steeped in financial depression, inflation was rampant, state currencies were worthless, and the trade deficit was absolutely staggering. America was literally on the brink of disaster. And people like James Madison and Alexander Hamilton knew it all too well.

It was time for the freedom lovers to reconvene and decide what course of action they would take. May of 1787 couldn't come fast enough, as that is when the delegates of 12 states would meet to decide whether the Articles of Confederation would be scrapped or merely amended.

Lesson

1. Create a Constitution: If you were designing a constitution, what powers would you confer on the government? Would you create a system of federalism (a system of government in which power is divided between the federal government and various regional governments) or a more unitary, centralized government? How would you ensure that the provisions contained in your constitution are not violated?

2. Money and Power: Participants will make simple choices involving actual dollars. Their decisions will illustrate the philosophical and practical problems that caused the fail-

ure of the Articles of Confederation. Afterward, the participants should discuss and describe the problems with the Articles and the best way to cure them.

Students will:

a. Note the historical analogy of 13 participants and 13 states.

b. Note the trade-off between the desire for the common good and the individual good.

c. Note that the voluntary nature of the Articles of Confederation is based on a flawed assumption that everyone will work for a common good.

d. Use the exercise to facilitate a discussion about specific historical events which impacted the government under the Articles of Confederation

General Instructions for Participants:

You are about to participate in an experiment designed to give you insight into the nature of government run by human beings. At the end of the experiment, you will receive a cash payment. The amount of the payment will depend partly on a decision that you make and partly on the decisions made by the other participants in your group.

During the experiment, you may not speak to any of the other participants. After the experiment is over, you are encouraged to discuss it with the other participants, but you are not required to reveal your decision to anyone. You will receive your payment in private. You can also be assured that the experiment involves no deception of any kind.

Decisions and Payoffs

On a piece of paper, indicate a choice of either RED or BLUE. The table below indicates how your choice and the choices of others in your group determine your pay-off. If you study the table carefully, you will notice that participants choosing "red" are always paid $1.75 more than those choosing "blue" no matter how many in the group choose "red." You will also notice that the payoff for the group as a whole drops as more participants choose "red." An individual is better off choosing "red," but if everyone chooses "red," then everyone is worse off than if everyone chooses "blue."

# in Group		Pay off		
Blue	Red	Blue	Red	Total Payout
13	0	$3.00	$0	$39.00
12	1	$2.75	$4.50	$37.50
11	2	$2.50	$4.25	$36.00
10	3	$2.25	$4.00	$34.50
9	4	$2.00	$3.75	$33.00
8	5	$1.75	$3.50	$31.50
7	6	$1.50	$3.25	$30.00
6	7	$1.25	$3.00	$28.50
5	8	$1.00	$2.75	$27.00
4	9	$ .75	$2.50	$25.50
3	10	$ .50	$2.25	$24.00
2	11	$ .25	$2.00	$22.50
1	12	$ .0	$1.75	$21.00
0	13	$ .0	$1.50	$19.50

Discussion Questions

1. During what time period did the Articles of Confederation exist?

2. What are the defining characteristics of the Articles of Confederation?

3. What are the Articles of Confederation's strengths and weaknesses?

4. How would you rate the overall effectiveness of the Articles of Confederation?

5. How did the Articles of Confederation impact the various groups of society at the time of its existence?

6. What major characteristics of the Articles of Confederation resulted in its demise and inspired the framers to create the Constitution?

7. Looking back, which do you believe was more appropriate for purposes of protecting freedom, the U.S. Constitution or the Articles of Confederation? Why?

Chapter 12
Convention of Delegates in 1787

"From such an assembly can a perfect production be expected? It therefore astonishes me, Sir, to find this system approaching so near to perfection as it does."
~Benjamin Franklin

As a result of the problems created by the Articles of Confederation in governing the United States, James Madison and Alexander Hamilton pushed for a convention, which would take place from May 14 to September 17, 1787 in Philadelphia, Pennsylvania.

The purported reason for the Convention was to revise and modify the Articles of Confederation. However, Madison and Hamilton recognized the inherent flaws in the Articles of Confederation and intended to create a new form of government. George Washington was appointed to preside over the Convention, and, after four months of intense and vigorous debate, the United States Constitution was proposed and adopted.

There were a number of contentious disputes during the Convention revolving around various issues, including:

1. The composition and election of the Senate and the House of Representatives;

2. The definition of "proportional representation" and whether to include slaves or other property;

3. Whether to divide the executive power among three persons or concentrate the executive power in a single president;

4. How to elect the president;

5. How long the president's term should be and whether he could stand for reelection;

6. What offenses would justify impeachment;

7. Slavery and its disposition, including the nature of a fugitive slave clause;

8. Whether to allow the abolition of the slave trade; and

9. Whether judges should be chosen by the legislature or executive.

Two factions existed at the Convention, namely the Federalists and Anti-federalists. Let's take a moment to talk about the different perspectives of each one. First, though, it is important to understand that, although the Federalists and Anti-federalists disagreed on some things, they did share certain core values. They both agreed that the greatest threat to the future of America revolved around the government's potential to abuse any power it was given until it made the people subjects. Having just experienced tyranny first-hand under the rule of Britain, they were slow to adopt any system of government.

Although they found common ground in their concern for tyranny, those similarities stopped there. Anti-federalists believed the proposed Constitution threatened to lead the United States down a path of corruption. All three branches of the new central government threatened the Anti-federalists' traditional belief in the importance of restraining government power.

The Federalists believed that the Constitution was necessary to safeguard the preservation of liberty and independence that came through the American Revolution. While the Federalists had developed a new political philosophy, they saw their most important role as defending the social gains of the Revolution. As James Madison said, the Constitution was designed to be a "republican remedy for the diseases most incident to republican government."

Critical to the discussion at the Convention were the powers of the legislature, executive, and judiciary. In large part, Madison had written, and Edmund Randolph presented, the Virginia plan, which the delegates worked from to create the final product. A Committee of Detail assembled in order to produce a working draft. Much of the draft remained in place. The Committee on Style produced the final version, and it was voted on. Thirty-nine of the delegates signed the Constitution, and it was then sent to the states for ratification.

One of the more animated debates that revolved around the ratification of the Constitution was the lack of a Bill of Rights. George Mason, Elbridge Gerry, and Edmund Randolph would not put their hand to the Constitution unless it contained additional protections to our fundamental liberties. Eventually a Bill of Rights would be adopted and ratified, but it wouldn't be until 1791. We'll take this up in more detail in Chapter 23.

Pursuant to Article VII of the Constitution, it was required that nine of the thirteen states ratify before the Constitution would carry the force of law. One of the mechanisms used to persuade the various states to unify in ratifying the Constitution was the Federalist Papers.

Eighty-five articles were written by James Madison, Alexander Hamilton, and John Jay, which, in turn, were printed in newspapers. Each of them wrote under the pseudonym of Publius. The Federalist Papers addressed the original intent and the reasons why a move from the Articles of Confederation to the newly-written Constitution was in the best interest of the country.

The first nine states to ratify the Constitution were as follows:

1. Delaware – December 7, 1787
2. Pennsylvania – December 12, 1787
3. New Jersey – December 18, 1787
4. Georgia – January 2, 1788
5. Connecticut – January 9, 1788
6. Massachusetts – February 6, 1788
7. Maryland – April 28, 1788
8. South Carolina – May 23, 1788
9. New Hampshire – June 21, 1788

The final four states would ratify on the following dates:
10. Virginia - June 25, 1788
11. New York - July 26, 1788
12. North Carolina - November 21, 1789
13. Rhode Island - May 29, 1790

The ratification of the Constitution was truly a great moment. The correlation between the Constitution and the Declaration of Independence is indisputable; they went hand-in-hand.

The Declaration of Independence was drafted in 1776. The Constitution came about in 1787.

The Declaration of Independence is the "why" of America's political system. The Constitution is the "how."

The Declaration of Independence is the promise. The Constitution is the fulfillment.

The Declaration of Independence established independence. The Constitution established nationhood.

The Declaration of Independence acknowledged and guaranteed liberty. The Constitution was structured to protect the fundamental freedoms of the people.

The Declaration of Independence spoke of liberty. The Constitution set forth the relationship between power and freedom.

The Declaration of Independence was the idealistic concept grounded in a set of convictions about the way the world should be. The Constitution is realistic and arranged power in such a way as to allow people to prosper, in spite of their natural depravities and human foibles.

The Declaration of Independence identifies individual rights as the core of the American way. The Constitution recognizes personal responsibilities and the boundaries of government.

The Declaration of Independence is what the founders were

willing to die for. The Constitution is what they were willing to live for. What are we willing to do to protect these charters of freedom?

Lesson

1. Divide into two groups. One group must defend the anti-federalist position of more power to the state governments. The second group must defend the federalist position and why a federal government with more power than granted under the Articles of Confederation is necessary.

2. Exercise caution (Adult supervision recommended): Using a beaver or coyote trap, illustrate the purpose of the Constitution, which is to minimize the chances of tyranny affecting the citizenry. Simply engage the trap and use a pencil to hit the lever to snap the trap into place. Make this fun by using your audience to build this experience up. After the demonstration, make it clear that the "Constitution is a complex maze of booby traps designed to stop tyranny in its tracks." Lead a discussion about how tyranny can still exist even with a Constitution. Of course, the people are the ultimate guardians of the Constitution, and, when we stop protecting it because we don't know what's in it, tyranny will abound.

3. The founders were attempting to build a stronger central government. At the same time, they wanted to be sure that it did not become too powerful. Read each of the following statements below and determine if it was meant to limit the power of the federal government ("L") or if it was meant to strengthen the federal government ("S"). Come up with your own additional examples.

    a. The Bill of Rights guarantees that the government will protect the rights of individuals and the authority of the states. (L)

b. The federal government is divided into three branches to provide checks and balances. (L)

c. A federal government has specific enumerated powers and any powers not vested remains with the states and the people. (L)

d. Bicameral representation, where the people are to be represented through the House of Representatives and the states are to be represented through the Senate, will guarantee that neither the small states nor large states end up with too much power in the legislative branch. (S)

e. The federal government will have the power to coin money and regulate interstate trade. (S)

f. The power of the legislative branch of government to declare war. (S)

g. The president can be impeached. (L)

Discussion Questions

1. Was it necessary to eliminate the Articles of Confederation? Why?

2. What disadvantages may have existed by replacing the Articles of Confederation with the U.S. Constitution?

3. What advantages were created through the adoption of the U.S. Constitution?

4. What issues do you think were critical to address at the convention in 1787?

5. What are your thoughts on term limits and the length of each term of office?

6. How do the Declaration of Independence and the Constitution work together?

7. How does the Constitution work as a trap to tyranny? What is the role of the people in engaging the trap?

Chapter 13

Preamble of the U.S. Constitution

"Let our government be like that of the solar system. Let the general government be like the sun and the states the planets, repelled yet attracted, and the whole moving regularly and harmoniously in several orbits."
~John Dickinson

The Preamble to the Constitution is an introductory statement outlining the Constitution's fundamental purposes and overarching principles. The founding fathers outlined, through this preamble, their intentions as to the Constitution's meaning and its objective.

"We the People of the United States, in Order to form a more perfect Union, establish Justice, insure domestic Tranquility, provide for the common defence, promote the general Welfare, and secure the Blessings of Liberty to ourselves and our Posterity, do ordain and establish this Constitution for the United States of America."

A closer review of each specific provision of the Preamble clearly reveals what the framers intended.

"We the People of the United States...."

The people of the United States recognized their inherent and unalienable right to govern themselves (i.e., popular sovereignty) and, therefore created the Constitution for the reasons outlined in the Preamble. Notably, the states generally waived standard voting restrictions and allowed a rather broad class of citizens to vote for the delgates that would attend the ratifying convention.

"....in Order to form a more perfect Union,...."

To form a strong central government made up of a union of states that are joined together by a common purpose and motivation, namely freedom.

"....establish Justice,...."

To ensure equal and just treatment to every person through the principles of due process and fairness.

"....insure domestic Tranquility,...."

To ensure peace within America's borders.

"....provide for the common defence,...."

To protect the people of the United States against foreign and domestic enemies.

"....promote the general Welfare,...."

To meet the general needs of the country's population in order to allow the society to function free from government or even private interference. This clause, along with the "General Welfare" clause found in Article I, Section 8 of the Constitution, has been the cause of much controversy. The General Welfare clause was never intended to grant the federal government unlimited authority, but rather to ensure that any act was done with the purpose of ensuring a benefit to all and not to certain specified groups. James Madison summed it up best when he said, "With respect to the two words 'general welfare,' I have always regarded them as qualified by the detail of powers connected with them. To take them in a literal and unlimited sense would be a metamorphosis of the Constitution into a character which there is a host of proofs was not contemplated by its creators."

"....and secure the Blessings of Liberty to ourselves and our Posterity,...."

To ensure liberty from one generation from the next.

"....do ordain and establish this Constitution for the United States of America."

Just as the people have the power and ability to separate themselves from the bands of tyranny, so too, do the people have the power to establish a system of government that promotes freedom and responsibility among the people and those that govern.

We often forget to look at the purpose of the governing document before acting. An oversight is potentially dangerous, if not fatal to freedom's cause. If we are to ensure that government remains small and freedom abounds, having a government that follows the rules is critical and necessary.

Lesson

1. Give each person in your group an assignment to address each of the critical components of the Preamble. Describe the meaning of each and illustrate how this is an improvement on the Articles of Confederation.

    a. We the People

    b. In order to form a more perfect union

    c. Establish justice

    d. Insure domestic tranquility

    e. Provide for the common defense

    f. Promote the general welfare

    g. Secure the blessings of liberty to ourselves and our posterity

2. Memorize the Preamble

    a. "We the People of the United States, in Order to form a more perfect Union, establish Justice, insure domestic Tranquility, provide for the common defence, promote the general Welfare, and secure the Blessings of Liberty to ourselves and our Posterity, do ordain and establish this Constitution for the United States of America."

    b. There are three parts of the preamble.

    i. Source: We the People

    ii. Purpose: Form, Establish, Insure, Provide, Promote, and Secure

    iii. Action: Ordain and Establish

Discussion Questions

1. When the Preamble was written, who constituted "the people" in the 1780s? Is this distinction important or do the values embraced in the Preamble transcend individuals and the various demographics that existed at the time?

2. What are some of the improvements that you would suggest over the Articles of Confederation in order to make a "more perfect union"?

3. The founders used the word tranquility. What is the difference between a country that is tranquil versus one that is not?

4. What is the difference between one centralized government being responsible for protecting the states as compared to each individual state being responsible for its protection? Which approach maximizes the opportunity for the people to relish in freedom?

5. What does it mean to promote the general welfare?

6. If the Constitution is a basic set of laws of a government or of an organization, how is a constitution different from other laws, regulations, or rules of a government or organization?

7. How do we secure the blessings of liberty to ourselves and our posterity?

Chapter 14
U.S. Constitution Overview

"The preservation of the sacred fire of liberty,
and the destiny of the republican model of government,
are justly considered as deeply, perhaps as finally staked,
on the experiment entrusted to the hands
of the American people."
~George Washington

The Constitution was proposed and adopted in 1787 and ratified in 1788. In order for the Constitution to go into effect, it was necessary for nine of the thirteen states to ratify. In many states, the ratification of the Constitution was wildly contested because many states, especially the small states, did not want to give up their sovereignty, and they felt that by ratifying the Constitution they would become subjects of the larger states with larger populations. They were concerned that the Constitution would bring about the very thing that the colonists had just escaped years before, namely the tyranny of an overbearing, mammoth-like government body.

As a result of the concerns of many of the states, James Madison, Alexander Hamilton, and John Jay came together to write numerous newspaper articles to convince the states to adopt this Constitution. The articles became known as the Federalist Papers, with a total of 85 articles published.

Historian Richard B. Morris noted that the Federalist Papers are an "incomparable exposition of the Constitution, a classic in political science unsurpassed in both breadth and depth by the product of any later American writer." To understand the original intent of the Constitution, one must read the Federalist Papers and even the Anti-Federalist Papers, which outlined some of the concerns with ratifying the U.S. Constitution, along with the advantages and disadvantages.

The purpose of the Constitution is rather simple. It is a complex maze of booby traps designed to stop tyranny in its tracks. Defending and insuring against tyrannical impulses and preserving freedom were the two key primary objectives. We wanted people to be free while living in an orderly society. How does the Constitution do that? It does so in a few important and prominent ways.

1. It limits government authority. The Constitution tells the federal government what it can do and reminds government officials and representatives of what they must avoid as they exercise granted authority. For example, the federal government has the power to tax and spend pursuant to the provisions outlined in Article I. However, in exercising this power, the federal government could not create a law prohibiting one from speaking out against the tax laws. Why? Because the First Amendment tells Congress that it cannot make any laws that infringe on speech.

2. The Constitution guarantees a republican form of government, ensuring that the rights of all are protected. In other words, government officials take an oath to uphold and protect that Constitution, which includes the obligation to protect the rights of all people and not just the majority or their constituents.

3. The first ten amendments (the Bill of Rights) enumerates some of the rights of the people. If our rights come from the Creator, why is it necessary to enumerate the rights of the people in the Constitution? This question was vigorously debated by the framers. Ultimately, the answer is that history has shown that government must always be reminded of what rights the people have or it will generally tread over them. The government's purpose is to protect the rights of the people, and the Constitution tells the government, in part, what some of the more important rights are (e.g., speech, assembly, press, religion, arms, etc.)

4. The Constitution separates power and divides authority. Our founders recognized a profound truth, namely human beings are inclined to abuse power. As a result, not all power can be given to one individual or one body. To minimize the chance of tyrannical rule, separating power and duties was critical and is the primary reason why the Constitution provides for three branches of government.

The following is a brief outline of the main body of the Constitution, which includes Articles I through VII, but not the ensuing 27 amendments. The body of the Constitution illustrates where each branch of government derives its authority, the parameters of that authority, the supremacy of the Constitution, restrictions on and among the individual states, etc.

This outline is designed to be a general resource and guide for the reader. You should not feel overwhelmed as you look at this list. However, you should commit to memorizing seven simple provisions, namely what each Article discusses. As a starting point, the highlighted, emboldened portions are what you should commit to memory.

1. **Article I – Legislative Branch**

   a. Section 1 - Legislative Powers Vested in the House of Representatives and the Senate

   b. Section 2 – House of Representatives

   c. Section 3 – Senate

   d. Section 4 – Congressional Elections and Meeting Requirements

   e. Section 5 – Congressional Rules of Order

   f. Section 6 – Congressional Pay, Immunities, and Office Prohibitions

   g. Section 7 – Congressional Law-Making Procedures

   h. Section 8 – Enumerated Powers of Congress

   i. Section 9 – Congressional Prohibitions on Legislation

   j. Section 10 – State Prohibitions on Legislation

2. **Article II – Executive Branch**

    a. Section 1 - Executive Powers Vested in the President

    b. Section 2 - Powers of the Executive

    c. Section 3 - Reporting State of the Union, Resolving Congressional Disagreements, Diplomatic Relations, Faithful Execution of the Law

    d. Section 4 - Impeachment

3. **Article III – Judicial Branch**

    a. Section 1 - Judicial Authority Vested in the Federal Courts

    b. Section 2 - Jurisdiction Vested in the Federal Courts

    c. Section 3 - Treason

4. **Article IV – Relationships Among the States**

    a. Section 1 - Full Faith and Credit

    b. Section 2 - Privileges and Immunities, Extradition, and Treatment of Fugitive Slaves

    c. Section 3 - State Admission into the Union and Governance of U.S. Property

    d. Section 4 - Republican Form of Governmen

5. **Article V – Amendment Process**

6. **Article VI – Federal Debt, Supreme Law of the Land, and No Religious Test for Public Office**

7. **Article VII – Ratification Process**

Lesson

1. Read the Constitution (30-minute exercise)

2. Memorize the seven articles of the Constitution. It's easy!

First, write Article I, Article II, etc. on the board with a blank space next to each. Have the group discuss what each article addresses. For purposes of the first three articles, a helpful tool for memorizing is simply recalling "LEJ." Article I speaks to the legislative branch ("L"). Article II speaks to the executive branch ("E"). And Article III addresses the judicial branch ("J"). Venture out and come up with your own acronyms for memorizing all seven articles.

3. Look at Article I (Legislative), Article II (Executive), and Article III (Judicial) and discuss one grant of authority or job description each one of the articles grants or outlines to each branch of government. For example: Article I gives the legislative branch the power to regulate commerce. As an additional exercise, use the following quiz.

a. Which branch of government deals with the following?

1. Makes law regulating interstate commerce (L)

2. Faithfully executes and enforces the laws (E)

3. Hears court cases and applies the law (J)

4. Declares war (L)

5. Includes the president, vice president, and the cabinet (E)

6. Divided into the House and Senate (L)

7. Makes laws to punish pirates (L)

8. Ratifies treaties with other countries (L (Senate))

9. Establishes an army and navy (L)

10. Selected by the Electoral College (E)

11. Selected by popular vote (L)

12. Appoints Supreme Court Justices, federal judges, ambassadors, and cabinet members (E)

13. Approves presidential appointments (L (Senate))

14. Makes a State of the Union address each year (E)

15. Receives ambassadors (E)

Discussion Questions

1. What is the purpose of the Constitution?

2. How does the Constitution limit authority and attempt to prevent tyranny?

3. How many Articles are in the Constitution? Which Article speaks to the Legislative Branch? Executive Branch? Judicial Branch?

4. Would you change anything about our current Constitution?

5. Has our Constitution deviated from the founders' original intent? How?

6. Does the government exist for the sake of the individual or does the individual exist for the sake of the government? Explain.

7. As you review the various powers of the different branches, would you propose conveying any of the enumerated powers of one branch to one of the other branches? For example, the legislature has the power to call up the state militia to quell a national emergency. Would you propose giving that power instead to that of the executive or judicial branch? Why or why not?

Chapter 15
Separation of Powers

"The accumulation of all powers, legislative,
executive, and judiciary, in the same hands,
whether of one, a few, or many, and whether hereditary,
self-appointed, or elective, may justly be pronounced
the very definition of tyranny."
~James Madison

The founders recognized the importance of dividing power. Because history teaches that people in authority tend to abuse that power to the detriment of freedom, they established a Constitution to minimize the possibility of tyrannical impulses taking a foothold on America.

As we move forward with the freedom experiment, we have to answer the question, "Who gets to make the rules?" Should we have one person making and enforcing all of the rules, or should we have multiple people doing that? Do we divide our elected representatives into branches of government? If so, what would those branches consist of? How many people should be within each of the branches of government and what authority should they have?

This principle is easy to understand and is just plain common sense. Take a look around or think about people you associate with on a daily basis. There are a number of people you trust. People you would lend money because you know that they would pay you back. You might share a secret with them because you are confident that they would keep their word not to tell anyone. You know they wouldn't talk about you behind your back and that they would never tell a lie. However, would you agree to elect them to be the sole leader over your school, for example, if they were able decide when you came to school, went to the bathroom, when and what you ate, what classes you would take, what people you could hang out with, and on and on? Think about that for a moment. Would you be comfortable with that?

You probably wouldn't. Why? For the same reason that our founding fathers created three branches of government, namely the legislative, executive, and judicial. When you ensure that one man does not have all of the power, you minimize your chances of someone abusing his power and you also maximize the likelihood that you will retain your freedom.

So, you might give one of the students in your class the power to decide on the lunch menu, but you would give another student the power to decide when lunch break is, and yet another student the power to decide how long that lunch break is. Why? Because fairness is increased as we distribute power among multiple individuals.

Do you see the genius of our founding fathers? This is precisely what they did with our U.S. Constitution.

As previously noted, the three branches of government codified in the U.S. Constitution are the legislative, executive, and judicial. Each branch has a specific function.

1. Legislative—The primary function of the legislative branch is to write, debate, and pass bills, which are relayed to the President either to approve or veto.

2. Executive—The primary function of the executive branch is to enforce the laws of the land and act as the commander-in-chief.

3. Judicial—The primary function of the judicial branch is to apply the laws according the intent and purpose of the Constitution.

Ultimately, we divide and separate power and divide authority to ensure that no one leader goes on a "power trip." The genius of our founders set up a system that would minimize tyranny and maximize freedom in a constitutional republic, and it all revolves around placing limitations and checks on power.

Lesson

1. Handcuffs, Power and Liberty Object Lesson
   a. Take one participant and handcuff or tie his hands be-
      hind his back and then tell him to release himself. Of
      course, unless your participant is an escape artist, he
      will be helpless. However, what happens if others step
      in with a key to the handcuffs or untie the knots bind-
      ing his hands? What happens if others are willing to de-
      fend against the person who initially restrained the
      participant? What happens if the fourth branch of gov-
      ernment (i.e., the people) steps in and rejects govern-
      ment efforts to limit the freedoms of the people by
      showing up at the ballot box? This is why the doctrine
      of separation of powers is so important. Government's
      primary job is to protect the people's liberty. However,
      if one branch of government unduly restrains the peo-
      ple, the two other branches can step in and check the
      branch that is acting illegally. More than that, the peo-
      ple are the only checks on a government gone rogue.

2. Separation of Powers Debates
   a. Question: Who should have the power to declare war?
      1. Position A: The president should have the sole
         power to determine when war is necessary and
         should have the power to decide when military ex-
         ecution is appropriate.
      2. Position B: When war is an issue, no one branch of gov-
         ernment should have the sole decision-making power.
         This power is best shared among at least two branches
         of government.
   b. George Washington was a noble man of good character.
      At the time of the founding many were in favor of
      Washington maintaining the presidency until his death.
      1. Position A: If men are noble, we should appoint
         them for life to lead.
      2. Position B: No matter how noble a person is, no

person should retain the power to govern for a life term. He will inevitably be corrupted.

Discussion Questions

1. What are the benefits of dividing power among three branches of government? What are the disadvantages?

2. What are the general functions of each of the three individual branches of government?

3. What are your thoughts on the idea that people are inclined towards power and, once received, they often abuse it? Is this true? List some historical examples to support your view.

4. Can you conceive a situation where you would approve of one person possessing all of the power to make, administer, and the interpret the rules or the law?

Chapter 16
Positive Powers v. Negative Powers

"A wise and frugal government, which shall restrain men from injuring one another, which shall leave them otherwise free to regulate their own pursuits of industry and improvement, and shall not take from the mouth of labor the bread it has earned. This is the sum of good government, and this is necessary to close the circue of our felicities."
~Thomas Jefferson

Our Constitution is a document that contains both positive powers (i.e., outlining what the government is permitted to do) and negative powers (i.e., specifying what government cannot do). It is of vital importance for freedom to limit the power and authority of government. Why? Because if government's authority is not limited, its leaders will ultimately assume more power by making more laws that infringe on the liberties of the people and expand their power base. In short, government typically increases its power base at the expense of individual liberty. That is specifically what our Constitution is designed to prevent and what our founders identified as its primary objective.

A U.S. congressman once erroneously said that Congress is permitted to do anything so long as it is not forbidden in the U.S. Constitution. When pressed a bit about this false assumption, he then acknowledged that most of what Congress does is not explicitly authorized by the Constitution. He is wrong on the first count and, sadly, violates his oath on the second count.

The Constitution is clear as to the limited power granted to the government. The 10th Amendment specifically states that "[t]he powers not delegated to the United States [federal government] by the Constitution, ... are reserved to the

States respectively, or to the people." In other words, if a particular power or authority to act in a certain capacity is not specifically granted to the federal government, it has no authority to act in that capacity. Instead, such non-enumerated powers are retained by the states and the people.

In summary, the Constitution tells the federal government specifically what it is permitted to do, but also tells it what traps it must avoid while performing legitimate governmental functions. Read the previous sentence again! This concept of positive and negative powers is beautiful, and the Constitution addresses the issue remarkably well.

So, what are some examples of positive powers and negative powers outlined in our Constitution? Let's take a look at just a few examples.

1. Positive Powers (What Government is Permitted to Do)
   a. Legislative Branch (Article I)
      1. Make laws pertaining to naturalization and the standards for acquiring citizenship.
      2. Tax and spend in order to provide for the protection of the country.
      3. Make laws in order to ensure that commercial products can move with ease across state lines.
      4. Declare war
      5. Coin money
      6. See Article I (Specifically, Section 8) of the Constitution for more examples.
   b. Executive Branch (Article II)
      1. Enforce the laws that are appropriately passed by the legislative branch.
      2. Lead our military forces as commander-in-chief.
      3. Engage in foreign diplomatic relations.
      4. See Article II of the Constitution for more examples.

c. Judicial Branch (Article III)

    1. Hear cases involving federal law or cases where the Constitution is implicated.

    2. Hear cases involving ambassadors, consuls, public ministers.

    3. See Article III of the Constitution for more examples.

2. Negative Powers (What Government is Not Permitted to Do)

a. Congress may not make laws that infringe on one's right to speak, practice religion, or assemble. (First Amendment)

b. The government may not make laws that infringe on the people's right to keep and bear arms. (Second Amendment)

c. The executive branch may not search one's property unless accompanied by a warrant or, in some cases, simply the presence of probable cause. (Fourth Amendment)

d. An individual may not be punished by the government for an alleged criminal act unless the person is first afforded a fair trial, a public trial, a speedy trial, and other due process protections. (Sixth Amendment)

e. Congress may not make a law that punishes a person retroactively for something that was legal at the time the act was committed. (Article I, Section 9)

f. See Article I, Sections 9 and 10, Article IV, and the Bill of Rights for additional examples.

Lesson

1. Illustration: You are sitting in a restaurant, and you decide you want to change the arrangements of the tables, paint the walls, and alter the menu. A person could only do this if he had explicit authority to do so (positive power). Once power is given (in this case, painting), some restriction may be placed on your work. For example, you can

paint the restaurant any color but red (negative power), free-standing tables are ok (positive power) but booths are prohibited (negative power), and the menu may not be changed to serve hamburgers and hot dogs (negative power). Use this illustration wherever you are and change the options in order to illustrate positive versus negative powers.

2. Create a list and lead a discussion about positive versus negative powers. On the left-hand side, list "positive powers," and on the right-hand side list "negative powers." Have members of your group list a power or prohibited action and whether it is positive or negative. Have them explain why. Alternatively, as the person leading the discussion, name a power or prohibited action and have the group decide what kind of power it is.

Discussion Questions

1. Why is it important to limit the powers of government?

2. Are there any circumstances where you would consider giving unlimited power in a particular area of the law to the government? War? Enforcement of the law? National security?

3. What is wrong with the following statement: "I am authorized to enact any piece of legislation so long as the Constitution does not forbid it."

4. Is it necessary to list both positive powers and negative powers in a ruling document such as the Constitution? Why or why not?

Chapter 17
The Creation of Law:
Legislative Branch (Article I)

"Freedom of men under government is to have a standing rule to live by, common to every society, and made by the legislative power vested in it."
~John Locke

Article I of the Constitution addresses the legislative powers, rules, and conduct of Congress, which consists of two chambers—the House of Representatives and the Senate. Article I is the operation's manual for those acting within the legislative branch of government.

In a nutshell, the Constitution grants Congress the sole authority to enact legislation, declare war, and to confirm or reject presidential appointments, along with substantial investigative powers.

House of Representatives and the Senate

The first chamber is the House of Representatives, which is made up of 435 elected members. Those 435 members are divided among the fifty states in proportion to their total population. The presiding officer of the chamber is the Speaker of the House who is elected by its members. According to the Constitution, members of the House are elected every two years and must be twenty-five years of age, a citizen of the United States for at least seven years, and a resident of the state they represent.

The second chamber is the Senate, which is comprised of 100 senators—two from each state. Until the ratification of the Seventeenth Amendment in 1913, senators were chosen by the state legislatures. The Seventeenth Amendment mandates that senators are elected by popular vote of the citizens of each state. Senators must be thirty years of age and a citizen of the United States for nine years. Senators are elected for six-year terms, which are staggered so that approximately one-third of the Senate is up for reelection every two years.

Although the Vice-President is a member of the executive branch, he also serves as President of the Senate and may cast the decisive vote in the event of a tie in the Senate.

Legislative Process

In order to pass legislation and submit it to the President for his approval, both the House and the Senate must pass the same bill by a majority vote. If the President vetoes a bill, Congress may override the veto by passing the bill again with at least a two-thirds majority in both the Senate and the House.

The first step in the legislative process is the introduction of a bill to Congress. Anyone can author the bill, but only members of Congress can introduce legislation. Some important bills are traditionally introduced at the request of the President. During the legislative process, however, the initial bill may undergo drastic changes.

After being introduced, a bill is referred to the appropriate committee for review. There are a number of House and Senate committees and subcommittees that oversee various policy areas.

Once a bill is submitted to a subcommittee, members may accept, amend, or reject it entirely. If the subcommittee agrees to move a bill forward, it is reported to the full committee, where the process is repeated again. Throughout this process, the committees and subcommittees call hearings to investigate the merits and flaws of the bill. They invite (and sometimes even compel through their subpoena power) experts, advocates, and opponents to appear before the committee and provide testimony regarding the matters at issue. As you can tell, this is an intense, deliberative process.

If the full committee votes to approve the bill, it is reported to the floor of the House or Senate, and the majority party leadership decides when to place the bill on the calendar for consideration. If a bill is particularly pressing, it may be considered immediately. Others may wait for months, and others may never be scheduled.

The House has a very structured debate process that takes place when a bill comes up for consideration. Each member who wishes to speak only has a few minutes. In the Senate, however, debate on most bills is unlimited. Senators may propose amendments to the bill under consideration and also may speak to other issues unrelated to the bill being considered. A senator may effectively delay the vote on a bill under consideration by staying on the floor and speaking for an extended period of time, a procedure called "filibuster." A vote by a supermajority of sixty senators can break a filibuster by invoking cloture and forcing a vote on the bill at issue. Once the debate is over, the vote of a simple majority passes the bill.

A bill must pass both the House and the Senate before it goes to the President for his review. Though the Constitution requires that the two bills from each chamber have the same wording, it rarely happens in practice. To bring the bills into alignment, a Conference Committee is convened, consisting of members from both chambers. The members of the committee produce a conference report, intended as the final version of the bill. Each chamber then votes again to approve the conference report. If approved, the bill is then sent to the President.

Upon receipt of a bill from Congress, the President has several options. If the President approves the bill, he may sign it into law, and the bill is then printed. If the President does not approve of the bill, he may veto it. If the bill is vetoed, it is sent back to Congress. Congress may override the veto with a two-thirds vote of both the Senate and the House, at which point the bill becomes law.

There are two other options that the President may exercise. If Congress is in session and the President takes no action within ten days, the bill becomes law. If Congress adjourns before the ten days are up and the President takes no action, then the bill dies and Congress may not vote to override. This is called a pocket veto, and if Congress still wants to pass the legislation, they must begin the entire process again when Congress reconvenes.

Overview of Article I

Let's look at a general overview of Article I of the Constitution. Note that not only does it outline what the legislative branch is permitted to do, it also lists specific prohibitions. The following is a general outline of the principles and objectives of Article I and its various sections.

Section 1 - "All legislative powers herein granted...."

1. All legislative powers are vested in Congress.

2. The legislature has the duty of enacting laws.

3. Congress is made up of two separate bodies, namely the Senate and the House of Representatives.

Section 2—House of Representatives

1. Represention according to population and elected by the people every two years.

2. Members of the House of Representatives must be:
   a. 25-years old
   b. A citizen of the United States for at least seven years.
   c. An inhabitant of the state in which they are elected at the time of the election.

3. A census is taken every ten years to determine apportionment of State representatives within the House.

4. The House has the sole power of impeachment.

Section 3—Senate

1. The Senate is comprised of two senators from each state, elected by the people for six-year terms.

2. Initially, senators were appointed by the state legislatures. However, since the ratification of the Seventeen Amendment in 1913, senators have been elected by popular vote.

3. Senators must be:
   a. 30-years old
   b. A citizen of the United States for at least nine years.
   c. A resident of the state in which they are elected at the time of the election.

4. Vice President of the United States is the President of the Senate but may only vote when there is a tie.

5. Senate has the sole power to try impeachment cases. In cases where the President is subject to impeachment, the Chief Justice shall preside.

Section 4—Elections and Meetings for Both Houses

1. The time, place, and manner of congressional elections are determined by state legislatures.

2. Congress must meet at least once annually.

Section 5—Rules for Each House

1. Each House may establish its own rules with certain limitations.

2. Each chamber may punish its members for certain disorderly conduct.

3. Adjournment of more than three days may only happen with the consent of both chambers.

Section 6—Rights and Duties of Congressman

1. Paid annually from the national treasury.

2. Privileged from arrest unless a felony, treason, or breach of the peace is committed.

3. Freedom of speech is enhanced for congressmen through immunity protection while on the floor or in a committee hearing.

4. May not hold any other civil office under the authority of the United States.

Section 7—Procedure for Making Laws

1. Bills pertaining to raising revenue must originate in the House of Representatives.

2. Every bill must pass through the House of Representatives and the Senate.

3. The President may sign or veto the bill. If vetoed, the bill returns to the originating chamber.

4. Two-thirds of both Houses may override a presidential veto.

5. Votes must be recorded in a public journal.

Section 8—Enumerated Powers of Congress

1. Tax and Spend—May only tax and spend for the general welfare and to provide for the common defense.

2. Borrow money on the credit of the United States.

3. Regulate Interstate commerce and commerce with foreign nations and Indian tribes.

4. Naturalization—Congress defines the process by which immigrants from foreign countries become citizens.

5. Regulates bankruptcy

6. Coins and regulate the value of money

7. Standardize weights and measures

8. Punish counterfeiting

9. Establish a postal system

10. Copyright and patent

11. Establish inferior federal courts

12. Punish crimes on the high seas

13. Declare war

14. Raise and finance armed forces

15. Establish rules for armed forces

16. Call up state militias

17. Congress may federalize state militias

18. Administer the seat of the government (Washington, D.C.)

19. Administer federal lands

20. Necessary and Proper - Pass laws that are critical to implementing any of the above powers.

Section 9—Powers Forbidden to Congress

1. May only suspend writs of Habeas Corpus in cases of rebellion or invasion.

2. Bills of Attainder and Ex Post Facto laws

3. Export taxes

4. Titles of nobility

Section 10—Powers Forbidden to the States

1. Treaties and alliances

2. Grant letters of marquee and reprisal

3. Coin money

4. Emit bills of credit

5. Bill of Attainder

6. Ex post facto

7. Impairing the obligation of contracts

8. May not impose export or import taxes

9. War unless invaded

Lessons

1. The following is a list of legislative powers. Lead a discussion and have the participants give a thumbs up or down depending on whether the legislature actually has the power. Continue to create your own list of questions by looking to Article I, Section 8.

   a. Congress can pass any law it wants to? (False)

   b. Congress can tax for purposes of national defense? (True)

   c. Congress has the power to impeach the governors of the states? (False)

   d. Congress creates federal courts such as district and appellate courts? (True)

   e. Congress cannot regulate interstate commerce? (False)

   f. Congress has no power to establish post offices. This is a state power? (False)

   g. Congress has the power to establish the army and navy? (True)

   h. Congress cannot make any laws about immigration? (False)

   i. Congress can make any law as long as it is "necessary and proper?" (False)

2. Memorize the powers of Congress, as outlined in Article I, Section 8

   a. TCC-NCC-PCC PAWN MMRRN

i. Taxes

ii. Credit

iii. Commerce

iv. Naturalization and Bankruptcy

v. Coinage

vi. Counterfeiting

vii. Post Office

viii. Copyright

ix. Courts

x. Piracy

xi. Army

xii. War

xiii. Navy

xiv. Militia

xv. Money for Militia

xvi. Rules for D.C.

xvii. Rules for Federal Land

xviii. Necessary and Proper

Discussion Questions

1. What is the job of the legislative branch?

2. What are the constitutional requirements in order to become a senator? A member of the House of Representatives? Are there any you would add or remove?

3. Do you agree that the House of Representatives should be established through proportional representation of the states (i.e., the more citizens in a state, the more representation in the House of Representatives)? What are the advantages and disadvantages of proportional representation?

4. Do you agree that each state should receive two senators

and no more and no less? What are the advantages and disadvantages?

5. How do the Senate and the House of Representatives check one another?

6. As you review the powers of the legislative branch, are there any that you believe should remain primarily with the states? Are there any powers that you would grant to the federal government that are not listed?

7. The national treasury ultimately pays members of Congress. Do you agree with this or do you believe that the states should determine their salary? Why or why not?

Chapter 18
The Sword of the President: Executive Branch (Article II)

"The contest, for all ages, has been to rescue Liberty from the grasp of executive power."
~Daniel Webster

The job of those in the executive branch, including the President, is to enforce the laws passed by the legislature. Their job is not to make law or even interpret the meaning of the law (outside of confirming its constitutionality). Instead, they are to enforce the law equally, fairly, and without bias or prejudice.

The power of the executive branch is vested in the President of the United States, who also acts as the Head of State and commander-in-chief of the armed forces. The President is responsible for implementing and enforcing the laws written by Congress and, to that end, appoints the members of his Cabinet and the heads of other federal agencies. The Vice President is also part of the executive branch, ready to assume the presidency should the need arise.

The cabinet and independent federal agencies are responsible for the day-to-day enforcement and administration of federal laws. These departments and agencies have specific missions and responsibilities.

Under Article II of the Constitution, the President is responsible for the execution and enforcement of the laws enacted by Congress. The President has the power either to sign legislation into law or to veto bills passed by Congress. However, Congress may override a veto with a two-thirds vote of both houses. The executive branch conducts diplomacy with other nations, and the President has the power to negotiate and sign treaties, which also must be ratified by a two-thirds vote of the Senate. The President can issue executive orders, which provide directives to executive officers or clarify laws.

The President also has the power to extend pardons and clemency for federal crimes, except in cases of impeachment.

With powers come several responsibilities, among them, as set forth in Article II, Section3, a constitutional requirement to "from time to time give to the Congress Information of the State of the Union, and recommend to their Consideration such Measures as he shall judge necessary and expedient." Although the President may fulfill the requirement in any way he chooses, presidents have traditionally given a State of the Union address to a joint session of Congress each January (except in inaugural years) outlining the agenda for the coming year.

The Constitution lists only three qualifications for the Presidency—the President must be thirty-five years of age, must be a natural born citizen, and must have lived in the United States for at least 14 years. And though millions of Americans vote in a presidential election every four years, the President is not, in fact, directly elected by the people. Instead, on the first Tuesday in November of every fourth year, the people elect members of the Electoral College ("Electors") for their respective states. Electors are apportioned to each of the fifty states by population—one for each member of their congressional delegation in the Senate and the House (with the District of Columbia receiving three votes) for a total of 538 electoral votes. These electors vote for and, effectively, elect the President.

The primary responsibility of the Vice President of the United States is to be ready at a moment's notice to assume the presidency if the President is unable to perform his duties. This can be due to the President's death, resignation, or temporary incapacitation, or in the event that the Vice President and a majority of the cabinet determine that the President is no longer able to discharge the duties of the presidency.

The Vice President is elected with the President by the

Electoral College—each elector casts one vote for President and another for Vice President. Before the ratification of the Twelfth Amendment in 1804, electors only voted for President, and the presidential candidate who received the second greatest number of votes became the Vice President.

The Vice President also serves as the President of the United States Senate. As such, when the Senate is "equally divided" on a vote, the Vice President casts the deciding vote. Except in the case of tiebreaking votes, the Vice President rarely presides over the Senate. Instead, the Senate selects one of its own members, usually junior members of the majority party, to preside over the Senate on a day-to-day basis.

Interestingly, the Constitution's framers gave little attention to the executive branch of government. The powers and scope of the executive's authority were defined rather quickly and with very little debate. On the other hand, the framers spent an incredible amount of time discussing and debating the powers of Congress.

The lack of attention paid to the executive branch may have been due to the delegates' unwillingness to see anyone other than George Washington sitting in the presidential chair. It seemed as though most assumed that Washington would indeed be the country's first president.

In Article II of the Constitution, the framers moved forward with a novel idea: a chief executive whose power came from the people rather than by heredity or force. The Constitution, however, provides little indication that the president would become as powerful as he has in modern times.

The framers obviously assumed that the legislative branch would be much more influential as a check on the power of the executive branch. James Madison wrote that it would "rarely if ever happen that the executive constituted as ours is proposed to be would have firmness enough to resist the legislature." Among the delegates, only Alexander Hamilton strongly advocated an executive with the power to match the monarchs of Europe.

In summary, the requirements of, and the powers delegated to, the executive branch under Article II, include the following.

Section 1—Power and Authority of the President

1. Establishes the office of the President and the Vice-President and sets their terms to be four years.

2. Presidents are elected by the Electoral College, in which each state has one vote for each member of Congress.

3. Originally, the President was the person with the most electoral votes and the Vice-President was the person with the greatest number of votes after the President-elect. However, this was later changed by the Twelfth Amendment.

4. To be the President, one must be at least thirty-five years old, must be a natural born citizen of the United States, and must have lived in the United States for at least fourteen years.

5. The President is paid a salary, which cannot be changed as long as he is in office.

Section 2—Commander-in-Chief and Director of the Executive Branch

1. The President is the commander-in-chief of the armed forces.

2. The President has a cabinet to advise and assist him.

3. The President may pardon criminals.

4. The President has the power, with the approval of the Senate, to make treaties with other nations.

5. The President appoints many of the judges and other members of the government, subject to Senate approval.

Section 3—Actions of the Executive

1. The President is to give a state of the union address.

2. The President is to make suggestions to Congress.

3. The President is to act as the head of state by receiving ambassadors and other heads of state.

4. The President is to ensure that the laws of the United States are "faithfully executed" and carried out.

Section 4 - Impeachment

The President, Vice President, and other federal officers may be impeached for "Treason, Bribery, and other high Crimes and Misdemeanors."

Lesson

1. Debate: The founders contemplated the number of presidents that we should have. One suggestion was that we should have three presidents, but they ultimately agreed on one. What are the advantages and disadvantages to having one president as compared to multiple presidents sitting at one time?

2. The following are the essential powers of the President, as the head of the executive branch. Commit this list to memory.

   a. Serves as commander-in-chief of all U.S. armed forces

   b. Commissions officers of the armed forces

   c. Grants pardons and reprieves from federal offenses (except impeachments)

   d. Convenes special sessions of Congress

   e. Receives foreign ambassadors

   f. Takes care that federal laws are faithfully executed

g. Wields the "executive power"

h. Appoints officials to lesser offices

3. Lead a discussion revolving around the following list of executive powers and have the participants give a thumbs up or down depending on whether the president actually has the specific power.

a. Defend and protect the Constitution? (True)

b. Draft laws and pass them? (False)

c. Commander-in-chief of the armed forces? (True)

d. Decide who wins court cases? (False)

e. Execute laws that have been passed that comply with the Constitution? (True)

f. Tell Congress what laws it must pass? (False)

g. Remove members of the U.S. Supreme Court who are not complying with the Constitution? (False)

h. Ask for advice from department heads? (True)

i. Negotiate treaties and approve them without approval from the other branches of government? (False)

j. Nominate Supreme Court justices? (True)

k. Nominate state legislators? (False)

l. Appoint a governor for each state? (False)

m. Approve or reject laws that have been passed by the legislature? (True)

n. Pardon a politician who has been impeached? (False)

o. Receive ambassadors from other countries? (True)

p. Declare war? (False)

q. Give a speech to Congress about the State of the Union? (True)

Discussion Questions

1. Identify the factors that you think were most important in leading to the concentration of power in the executive branch of today.

2. In your opinion, does the executive branch today have too much power relative to the other two branches of government? Why or why not?

3. Do you think any specific recent exercises of presidential power have been problematic? Would you remove or add to the powers of the President?

4. What are the constitutional requirements that must be met in order to become President? Are there any you would add or remove?

Chapter 19
The Power of the Courts: Judicial Branch (Article III)

"There is hardly a political question in the United States which does not sooner or later turn into a judicial one."
~Alexis de Tocqueville

While the executive branch is elected through the Electoral College and the legislative branch is elected by the people, members of the judicial branch are appointed by the President and confirmed by the Senate. It is important to have at least one branch of government that is anti-democratic in nature, i.e., not directly accountable to the people. And the reason is simple. We need to have an entity that will protect the rights of even those who hold minority views and where that same protection does not depend on the ballot box or what people think about the judicial decision. If judges were directly accountable to the people, their decisions may very likely hinge on the passions and inclinations of the general population.

Article III of the Constitution establishes the judicial branch as the third branch of government. Congress has significant discretion to determine the shape and structure of the federal judiciary. Even the number of Supreme Court justices is left to Congress, with the power to establish courts inferior to the Supreme Court. To that end, Congress has established the United States district courts and circuit courts of appeals. District courts hear most federal cases, civil and criminal, and the courts of appeals review cases appealed from the district courts.

Federal judges can only be removed through impeachment by the House of Representatives and conviction in the Senate. Federal judges do not serve fixed terms. Instead, they serve until their death, retirement, or impeachment and subsequent conviction by the Senate. By design, this is supposed to ensure that the justices are independent and are not influenced by the passions of the people. Judges are supposed to apply the law with only justice in mind, independent of electoral or political concerns.

Generally, Congress determines the jurisdiction of the federal courts. The Constitution provided that the Supreme Court shall have original jurisdiction (i.e., acts as a trial court) in certain types of cases, an authority that cannot be stripped by Congress. In all other cases, the Court has appellate jurisdiction.

Federal courts only hear actual cases and controversies. A party bringing a suit must show that it has been legally harmed. In other words, the courts do not issue advisory opinions regarding the constitutionality of laws or the legality of actions if the ruling would have no practical effect. Cases brought before the judiciary typically proceed from district court to appellate court and, in some cases, to the Supreme Court of the United States, although the Supreme Court hears comparatively few cases each year. The Supreme Court is the highest court in the land and the only arm of the federal judiciary specifically required by the Constitution.

Although the Supreme Court may hear an appeal on any question of law provided it has jurisdiction, it usually does not hold trials. Instead, the Court's task is to apply the Constitution, to decide whether a law is relevant to a particular set of facts, or to rule on how a law should be applied. According to Federalist No. 78, the federal courts have a duty to interpret and apply the Constitution and to disregard any statute that is inconsistent with the Constitution:

> *The interpretation of the laws is the proper and peculiar province of the courts. A constitution is, in fact, and must be regarded by the judges, as a fundamental law. It therefore belongs to them to ascertain its meaning, as well as the meaning of any particular act proceeding from the legislative body.*

As the U.S. Supreme Court makes its decisions, lower courts are obligated to follow the precedent. The concept known as *stare decisis* ("let the decision stand") allows for consistency in the application of the law across jurisidictions.

In almost all instances, the Supreme Court does not hear an appeal from a lower court as a matter of right. Instead, parties must petition the Court for a *writ of certiorari*. It is the Court's custom and practice to "grant cert" if four of the nine justices decide that they should hear the case. These are typically cases that the Court considers sufficiently important to review. A common example is when two or more of the federal courts of appeals have ruled differently on the same question of federal law or the Constitution.

Very few cases that petition to have their case reviewed by the Supreme Court are actually granted. However, if the petition is granted, each side will author legal briefs outlining their positions. The case will then be set for oral argument where each side will typically have 30 minutes to argue their case, subject to questions by the justices. Once arguments are completed, the justices often take months to issue their ruling.

Let's look at Article III of the Constitution and identify some of the powers of the judicial branch.

Section 1—Judicial Authority Vested in the Federal Courts

1. U.S. Supreme Court established
2. Lower federal courts established by Congress.
3. Judges hold their office subject to good behavior.

Section 2—Jurisdiction Vested in the Federal Courts

1. Types of cases the courts may hear.
2. Original versus Appellate jurisdiction
3. Jury trial preserved

Section 3—Treason

1. Requirement to prove treason and subsequent punishment. While the judicial branch is often criticized, few can argue that it is critical to maintaining a free society While the courts don't always get it "right," they have been been instrumental in moving the ideal of freedom forward.

Lesson

1. Supreme Court Simulation: Here we will experience what actually happens at the U.S. Supreme Court. This is a great exercise in a larger group setting. Pick three to five individuals to act as judges, and then divide the remaining people into two groups. Pick any issue (e.g., minimum wage, flag burning, etc.) and tell each side the position they will argue. While they may not agree with their position, they will begin the process of really learning to think critically about various issues. After each side has prepared, the participants will have the opportunity to argue their case in front of the appointed judges who will ask the participants' questions.

2. The following is a list of judicial powers. Lead a discussion and have the participants give a thumbs up or down depending on whether the judicial branch actually has the power.

   a. The Supreme Court acts primarily as an appellate court? (True)

   b. In some cases, the U.S. Supreme Courts acts as a trial court? (True)

   c. There are three justices on the U.S. Supreme Court? (False)

   d. The Supreme Court can strike down an unconstitutional law? (True)

   e. When a person faces criminal charges, the case will begin at the U.S. Supreme Court? (False)

f. The Supreme Court must take every case that is appealed to it? (False)

g. If you break a state law, your case will probably be in a state court system? (True)

h. The Supreme Court's power to apply the Constitution to legislative, executive, and judicial decisions is called judicial review? (True)

i. The appellate courts throughout the United States are specifically established by the Constitution? (False)

j. The U.S. Supreme Court has the power to overrule the lower courts? (True)

k. The inferior federal court system, which consists of district courts and courts of appeals, was created by Congress? (True)

l. State court systems were created by the Constitution of the United States? (False)

m. When you ask a higher court to review a case, you are making an appeal? (True)

n. When the court of appeals affirms a case, it sends the case back to the trial court for a new trial? (False)

o. The Supreme Court is established by the U.S. Constitution? (True)

3. Have each member of your group come up with two questions about the powers of the judicial branch. Quiz one another. For example: "The Supreme Court is the highest court in the land." (True)

Discussion Questions

1. Is judicial review a good idea? Should nine unelected justices be able to tell our elected representatives whether their enacted laws are constitutional or whether the President is behaving in line with the Constitution?

2. Are courts more likely to block an enlightened consensus

with their adherence to outdated principles or to protect the politically weak from oppressive majorities?

3. Are judges, protected with lifetime tenure and drawn generally from the educated class, more likely to be reflective and above the passing enthusiasms that drive legislative action?

4. Do legislators or members of the executive branch have any responsibility to judge the constitutionality of their own actions or is it only the Supreme Court that may make those decisions?

5. Could we have a workable system of government without judicial review?

6. There are no specific constitutional requirements in order to become a judge. Do you agree or disagree with the absence of any prerequisites? If you disagree, what would you add as a requirement?

Chapter 20
State's Power (Article IV)

"Whenever I use the word republic with approbation, I mean a government in which the people have collectively, or by representation, an essential share in sovereignty."
~John Adams

Although the Constitution was a document that was designed to address first and foremost the scope of the federal government's authority, there are a few sections that address state authority and establish parameters for certain actions related to the conduct of the various states. Article IV is one of those sections. Four sections are found in Article IV of the Constitution. We will proceed through each one.

Section 1. Full faith and credit

✦✦✦

Full Faith and Credit shall be given in each State to the public Acts, Records, and judicial Proceedings of every other State. And the Congress may by general Laws prescribe the Manner in which such Acts, Records and Proceedings shall be proved, and the Effect thereof.

✦✦✦

This section requires the states to extend "full faith and credit" to the public acts, records and court proceedings of other states. Congress may prescribe the manner in which such acts, records, or proceedings may be proven.

This means that if a married couple is divorced in Arizona and one of the parties is ordered to pay child support, that divorce and support decree will be recognized by California (or other state) authorities. The design of this provision is to ensure that the states do not act as independent sovereigns to the degree that would allow the citizens of one state to escape their legal obligations by fleeing to another state. Just as important, a state would not be permitted to disregard the records of another state.

Section 2. Privileges and Immunities

✦✦✦

The Citizens of each State shall be entitled to all Privileges and Immunities of Citizens in the several States.

✦✦✦

The first clause in Section Two of Article IV requires interstate protection of "privileges and immunities." The seeming ambiguity of the clause has given rise to a number of different interpretations. Some contend that the clause requires Congress to treat all citizens equally. Others suggest that citizens of states carry the rights accorded by their home states while traveling in other states.

Neither of these theories has been endorsed by the Supreme Court, which has held that the clause simply means that a state may not discriminate against citizens of other states in favor of its own citizens. In other words, the separate states may not discriminate against out-of-state residents, which includes the following:

1. Protection by the government;

2. The enjoyment of life and liberty;

3. The right of a citizen of one state to pass through or to reside in any other state for purposes of trade, agriculture, and professional pursuits;

4. To claim the benefits of the writ of habeas corpus;

5. To institute and maintain actions of any kind in the courts of the state;

6. To take, hold, and dispose of property; and

7. To equal treatment by the government in their enforcement of the law.

In short, marriages are acknowledged from state to state. If a suit is brought and settled in one state, the same lawsuit cannot be brought in another state. And if someone is found guilty of a crime in in one state, that guilt is recognized by the other states.

Extradition of Fugitives

+++

A Person charged in any State with Treason, Felony, or other Crime, who shall flee from Justice, and be found in another State, shall on demand of the executive Authority of the State from which he fled, be delivered up, to be removed to the State having Jurisdiction of the Crime.

+++

Fugitives from justice may be extradited on the demand of executive authority of the state from which they have fled. Article IV, Section 2 of the Constitution provides for the extradition of fugitives who have committed "treason, felony or other crime," which incorporates all acts prohibited by the laws of the state seeking extradition, including misdemeanors and small or petty offenses.

The motives of the governor of the state demanding the extradition may not be questioned. The accused cannot defend himself against the charges in the extraditing state but, instead, must do so in the state to which he is being extradited. However, the accused may prevent extradition by offering clear evidence that he was not in the state from which he allegedly fled at the time of the crime. There is no constitutional requirement that extradited fugitives be tried only for the crimes named in the extradition proceedings.

Fugitive Slave Clause

+++

No Person held to Service or Labour in one State, under the Laws thereof, escaping into another, shall, in

Consequence of any Law or Regulation therein, be discharged from such Service or Labour, but shall be delivered up on Claim of the Party to whom such Service or Labour may be due.

✦✦✦

When first adopted, this clause applied to fugitive slaves and required that they be extradited upon the claims of their enslavers, but it provided no means for doing so. The Fugitive Slave Act of 1793 created the mechanism for recovering a fugitive slave, overruled any state laws giving sanctuary, made it a federal crime to assist an escaped slave, and allowed "slave-catchers" into every state and territory of the United States.

In 1864, during the Civil War, an effort to repeal this clause of the Constitution failed. However, this clause was rendered essentially moot when the Thirteenth Amendment abolished slavery.

Section 3. New States

✦✦✦

New States may be admitted by the Congress into this Union; but no new State shall be formed or erected within the Jurisdiction of any other State; nor any State be formed by the Junction of two or more States, or parts of States, without the Consent of the Legislatures of the States concerned as well as of the Congress.

✦✦✦

Section 3 of Article IV provides that Congress may admit new states to the Union, except that no new state may be formed by joining multiple states without the consent of Congress and all state legislatures concerned.

The Constitution does not require that states be admitted on an "equal footing" with the original states. In fact, the Constitutional Convention rejected a proposal requiring the equality of new states. Nevertheless, Congress has included equality clauses in the statehood acts for the admission of new states. Congressional restrictions on the equality of states, even when those limitations have been found in the acts of admission, have been held void by the Supreme Court.

The question of seceding from the Union is not addressed in the Constitution. In *Texas v. White* (1869), the Supreme Court suggested that the Constitution ordained the "perpetuity and indissolubility of the Union." The Court did allow, however, some possibility of the divisibility "through revolution, or through consent of the States."

Federal property and the Territorial Clause

✦✦✦

The Congress shall have power to dispose of and make all needful Rules and Regulations respecting the Territory or other Property belonging to the United States; and nothing in this Constitution shall be so construed as to Prejudice any Claims of the United States, or of any particular State.

✦✦✦

The *Territorial* or the *Property Clause* in Article IV, Section 3 gives Congress the final power over every territory or other property of the United States. This clause also permits Congress to dispose of and legislate for all territories and properties belonging to the United States.

Section 4. Republican Form of Government

✦✦✦

The United States shall guarantee to every State in this Union a Republican Form of Government, ...

✦✦✦

This clause, sometimes called the Guarantee Clause, has historically been a part of the debate concerning the rights of citizens vis-a-vis state governments. The Guarantee Clause mandates that federal and state governments in the United States must be grounded in republican principles.

The Constitution does not explain what exactly constitutes a republican government. However, the Federalist Papers provide insight as to the intent of the Founders. A republican form of government is distinguished from a pure democracy, which the Founding Fathers wanted to avoid. As James Madison wrote in Federalist No. 10, "[h]ence it is that such [pure] democracies have ever been spectacles of turbulence and contention; have ever been found incompatible with personal security or the rights of property; and have in general been as short in their lives as they have been violent in their deaths."

Advocates contend that the Guarantee Clause prohibits the use of direct democracy procedures in the states. Ostensibly, this would preclude the use of the initiative, referendum, and recall measures because they are all tools of direct democracy that allow the electorate to exercise legislative power independently from their republican representatives.

Protection from Invasion and Domestic Violence

✦✦✦

... and [the United States] shall protect each of them [the States] against Invasion; and on Application of the Legislature, or of the Executive (when the Legislature cannot be convened) against domestic Violence.

✦✦✦

Article IV, Section 4 also requires that the United States protect each state from invasion and, upon the application of the state legislature (or executive, if the legislature cannot be convened), from domestic violence, internal invasion, or a societal uprising.

Lesson

Give the following quiz and discuss. Come up with additional questions to solidify your knowledge of Article IV.

1. Full Faith and Credit among the states means that:
   a. states respect as valid the legal judgments from the other states. (Correct)
   b. all states must have the same traffic and criminal laws on the books.
   c. states can give lines of credit to one another.

2. All citizens of the United States are entitled to:
   a. the right to vote in other states' elections.
   b. only follow the laws of their own state when in another state.
   c. all privileges and immunities of citizens of that state. (Correct)

3. If a person commits a crime in one state and flees from that state, the state to which the criminal has fled:
   a. can keep the accused criminal in that state and give him immunity.
   b. must return the accused criminal to the state where the crime was committed if requested. (Correct)
   c. can deport the accused criminal to any states of its choosing.

4. If a new state to be admitted to the union is formed within a current state or from two or more other states, it must be approved by:
   a. the President.
   b. the Supreme Court.
   c. the state legislatures involved and the Congress.

5. The United States government guarantees to the states:
   a. a democratic form of government and protection from invasion.
   b. a parliamentary form of government and protection

from invasion.

c. a republican form of government and protection from invasion.

Discussion Questions

1. What does Article IV cover?

2. If you get married in one state then move to another, do you have to get married again? Why not?

3. If you are convicted of a crime in your state, can you move to another state so you have no criminal record? Explain.

4. Can Texas tell those who are not citizens of the state they have to pay higher taxes to take advantage of the resources of the state? Explain.

5. What is extradition?

6. Do states have to extradite criminals or can they choose not to if they feel the requesting state is being unfair?

7. When slavery was legal, what had to happen to captured runaway slaves?

8. Is it possible for the United States to accept more states into the Union? How?

9. If a large city within the state wanted to break off and become its own state, could it? Explain.

10. If Vermont and New Hampshire wanted to become a single state, could they do so? Explain.

11. Puerto Rico is a territory of the United States. Do they have all the rights and responsibilities of the states?

12. Could Maine decide to appoint a queen to rule the state?

13. What happens if Florida is attacked or invaded?

Chapter 21
Amending the Constitution (Article V)

"Whatever be the Constitution, great care must be taken to provide a mode of amendment when experience or change of circumstances shall have manifested that any part of it is unadapted to the good of the nation"
~Thomas Jefferson

Article V of the Constitution reads as follows:

The Congress, whenever two thirds of both Houses shall deem it necessary, shall propose Amendments to this Constitution, or, on the Application of the Legislatures of two thirds of the several States, shall call a Convention for proposing Amendments, which, in either Case, shall be valid to all Intents and Purposes, as Part of this Constitution, when ratified by the Legislatures of three fourths of the several States, or by Conventions in three fourths thereof, as the one or the other Mode of Ratification may be proposed by the Congress; Provided that no amendment which may be made prior to the Year One thousand eight hundred and eight shall in any Manner affect the first and fourth Clauses in the Ninth Section of the first Article; and that no State, without its Consent, shall be deprived of its equal Suffrage in the Senate.

The authority to amend the Constitution is derived from Article V. The Constitution provides that an amendment may be proposed either by the Congress with a two-thirds majority vote in both the House of Representatives and the Senate or by an Article V convention called by two-thirds of the State legislatures. None of the twenty-seven amendments to the Constitution have been proposed through an Article V convention. Congress may propose an amendment in the form of a joint resolution. Since the President does not have a constitutional role in the amendment process, the joint resolution does not go to the White House for signature or approval.

The Constitution spells out four specific paths for a proposed amendment to officially become a part of the Constitution:

- Proposal by convention of two-thirds (2/3) of the states; ratification by three-fourths (3/4) of the state conventions. (Never utilized)

- Proposal by two-thirds (2/3) of the convention of states; ratification by three-fourths (3/4) of the state legislatures. (Never utilized)

- Proposal by two-thirds (2/3) of Congress; ratification by three-fourths (3/4) of the state conventions. (Used once)

- Proposal by two-thirds (2/3) of Congress; ratification by three-fourths (3/4) of state legislatures. (Used on multiple occasions)

While the most common method utilized under Article V has been for Congress to propose amendments, the states also have authority to propose amendments. If Congress proposes the amendment, each chamber (House and the Senate) must approve the amendment by a two-thirds vote. If the states wish to propose an amendment, two-thirds of the state legislatures must call on Congress to convene a convention.

Regardless of the method utilized to propose the amendment, it must always be ratified by and through the states. Three-fourths of the state legislatures or state conventions must approve the amendment. The proposed amendment becomes part of the Constitution as soon as it is ratified by three-fourths of the States (38 of 50 States).

In addition to specifying the means by which the Constitution may be amended, Article V forbids amendments that would repeal the language in Article I, Section 9, which prohibits a ban on the importation of slaves prior to 1808, or the language in Article I, Section 3, which provides for equal representation of the states in the Senate. The first prohibition was of limited duration and only restricted a constitutional amendment addressing this issue until 1808. The second prohibition—"no state, without its consent, shall be deprived of its equal Suffrage in the Senate"—was placed in the Constitution to protect the smaller states and ensure that their representation in the Senate was not any less than the larger states — every state has two senators regardless of their size.

Lesson

Give the following quiz and come up with additional questions as well:

1. The President may officially propose an amendment to the Constitution? (False)

2. If an amendment is initiated by Congress, both chambers (House and the Senate) must approve the proposed amendment by a two-thirds vote? (True)

3. The States always ratify proposed amendments but they can never propose an amendment? (False)

4. If both Congress and the states go through the appropriate process of amending the Constitution, an amendment to give the larger states five Senators and the smaller states three senators would be permissible? (False)

Debate: If the federal government does not appear to be adhering to the Constitution, will an amendment restricting further power make a difference? Why or why not? Divide your group into two groups and take opposing sides on whether an amendment to the Constitution is a good idea to address apparent government overreach. For example, consider the following issues:

1. Will term limits stop government's disregard of the Constitution?

2. Will clarification of the General Welfare clause or the Commerce clause reign in government's abuse of power?

3. Will abolishing the Seventeenth Amendment restore power back to the states?

Discussion Questions

1. What does Article V do?

2. Is it a good idea to allow for the Constitution to be amended? Can you name an example of an amendment that was particularly important to achieving our country's ideal of freedom?

3. Describe the process of amending the Constitution?

4. You will note that the people are never permitted to directly vote on amending the Constitution. Instead Congress or the states do so. What are the advantages and disadvantages of such a process? Should the people have a direct voice on the adoption of any amendment to the U.S. Constitution?

5. How is an amendment proposed?

6. Who can call an Article V convention?

7. What does ratify mean?

8. What happens if an Amendment is ratified?

9. Can the enactment of an amendment ever violate the "first principles" of the Constitution?

Chapter 22
The Constitution: Supreme Law of the Land (Article VI)

"Every law consistent with the Constitution will have been made in pursuance of the powers granted by it. Every usurpation or law repugnant to it cannot have been made in pursuance of its powers. The latter will be nugatory and void."
~Thomas Jefferson

Article VI of the Constitution is known as the "Supremacy clause" and, in pertinent part, reads as follows:

✦✦✦

This Constitution, and the Laws of the United States which shall be made in Pursuance thereof; and all Treaties made, or which shall be made, under the Authority of the United States, shall be the supreme Law of the Land; and the Judges in every State shall be bound thereby, any Thing in the Constitution or Laws of any State to the Contrary notwithstanding.

✦✦✦

Any federal system needs a strategy for dealing with potential conflicts between the federal and state governments. The Supremacy Clause is, in reality, a conflict-of-laws rule, which specifies that the Constitution and federal laws made in pursuance of the Constitution take priority over any state acts that conflict with the Constitution itself.

It is important to recognize that the Supremacy Clause does not grant power to any branch of the federal government. In addition, the Supremacy Clause does not distribute or allocate power between the federal and state governments. Instead the Constitution resolves any conflict between the federal and state governments once federal power has been validly exercised. The key word here is "validly." Just because government does something does not mean it was done legitimately. The Supremacy Clause is a straightforward interpretative rule that is directed to *all* legal interpreters, including members of Congress, federal executive officials, federal judges, state-court judges, or other state officials.

Under Article VI, treaties are dealt with differently from laws. There is a textual distinction in the "treaty" clause between laws "made in pursuance [of the Constitution]" and treaties "made under the authority of the United States." The language of Article VI does not in any way imply that treaties are "supreme" if they are not made in pursuance of the Constitution. The Supreme Court has declared that neither a treaty approved by the Senate nor an executive agreement made under the President's authority can create obligations that violate constitutional guarantees, such as those found in the Bill of Rights.

Here are a few thoughts from some our founders about the meaning of the Supremacy Clause of the Constitution:

Alexander Hamilton, at New York's convention: "I maintain that the word *supreme* imports no more than this — that the Constitution, and laws made in pursuance thereof, cannot be controlled or defeated by any other law. The acts of the United States, therefore, will be absolutely obligatory as to all the proper objects and powers of the general government…*but the laws of Congress are restricted to a certain sphere, and when they depart from this sphere, they are no longer supreme or binding*" (emphasis added).

In Federalist No. 33, Hamilton added: "It will not, I presume, have escaped observation that it expressly confines this supremacy to laws made pursuant to the Constitution…."

Thomas McKean, at the Pennsylvania convention, said, "The meaning [of the Supremacy Clause] which appears to be plain and well expressed is simply this, that Congress have the power of making laws upon any subject *over which the proposed plan gives them a jurisdiction*, and that *those laws, thus made in pursuance of the Constitution*, shall be binding upon the states" (emphasis added).

James Iredell, at the First North Carolina convention noted, "When Congress passes a law consistent with the Constitution, it is to be binding on the people. If Congress, under pretense of executing one power, should, in fact, usurp another, they will violate the Constitution."

No federal or state law, treaty, administrative law, municipal ordinance, or state constitution can supersede the Constitution. As Article VI makes clear, the Constitution is the supreme law of the land. While this principle is rather simple, the practical reality is that there is a constant struggle to decide what the Constitution means and whether the actions and conduct of the federal government and various government agencies conflict with the letter and spirit of the Constitution. Defending this charter of freedom is certainly not a spectator sport.

Lesson

1. Write each on of the following on slips of paper.
   a. U.S. Constitution
   b. Treaties
   c. Federal Law
   d. State Government
   e. County Government
   f. Municipal Government

   Although a bit oversimplified, this is a hierarchy of supremacy. Give each of the participants the slip of paper and then have each person publish their piece. The next person will have to decide whether their sheet of paper fits above or below those that have been listed. As you go through this exercise, it will no doubt elicit some debate. For example, is federal law really above state law? Only if the federal law has been enacted pursuant to the authority granted in the Constitution. In addition, can a city create a law that conflicts with state law? This exercise is one that is designed to help others understand the province of authority within the scope of each governmental entity.

2. Debate the following:
   a. The Jungle Country of Fruitzunia signs a treaty with the United States of America. The treaty says that fruitcake will be delivered to every home in the U.S. during the month of December. Georgia's state constitution prohibits the sale or consumption of fruitcake throughout the state during any given month. Who wins? As you contemplate which constitution should prevail, ask yourself whether the treaty is valid, whether Georgia's constitutional provision should be recognized in light of the fundamental principles of freedom, etc.? If you don't like the outcome, how can it be changed?

Discussion Questions

1. Why is it necessary to have a ruling document? What are the problems of not having a document that is the supreme law of the land?

2. Who should decide what the Constitution means? For example, the Fourth Amendment forbids "unreasonable searches and seizures." Who should decide what is "unreasonable"?

3. Why is it that an international treaty should not be able to trump the U.S. Constitution? What are possible consequences of allowing a treaty to have supreme status?

4. The Constitution makes it clear that federal laws "made

in pursuance" of the Constitution are supreme. What does it mean to be "made in pursuance thereof"?

5. What is the difference between the federal government and a state government?

6. Are the federal laws passed through U.S. Congress binding on a person living in any one of the states in the U.S.?

7. Are the provisions of the Constitution binding on a person living in any one of the states in the U.S.?

8. Do you think a state should be allowed to pass a law that conflicts with provisions of the U.S. Constitution? Why or Why not?

Chapter 23
The Bill of Rights and the Various Amendments

"A Bill of Rights is what the people are entitled to against every government, and what no just government should refuse, or rest on inference."
~Thomas Jefferson

The first ten amendments to the Constitution were all adopted (1789) and ratified (1791) collectively as the Bill of Rights. It is important to understand that the Bill of Rights, or any declaration of rights for that matter, does not give us our liberty or the rights enumerated therein. Those rights are inherent in us. Why then is a Bill of Rights even necessary?

That is the question raised on September 17, 1787, the day the delegates at the Philadelphia Convention approved of the text of the Constitution and agreed to send it to the states for ratification. On that day, 41 delegates met in the east room of Independence Hall to sign the Constitution. However, to the surprise of many, Colonel George Mason, along with a few others, refused to sign. When asked by James Madison why he would not sign the document that they had spent four months debating and drafting, Mason stated "[b]ecause it does not have a Bill of Rights." Madison, on the cusp of anger and desperation, replied, "but Colonel Mason, we have not given the federal government enough power to trample our rights." And Mason answered, "[b]ut they will, and they always do."

That conversation should make it clear that our framers did not believe our liberties come from the people, from government, or from a piece of paper. Instead, our status as human beings reveals this "self-evident" truth, and those liberties are always in danger by those in authority. As a result, ten amendments were ratified for one primary purpose—to put government on notice as to what we recognize as our freedoms, what they have an obligation to protect, and what they must steer clear of as they carry out various government functions.

The Bill of Rights notes three different types of protections:

1. The protection of certain fundamental liberties such as speech and the right to worship according to the dictates of one's own conscience.

2. The protection against the government as they attempt to deprive one of his or her liberty or property. For example, if a person violates another's liberty and takes his car, government may punish the perpetrator. However, before punishment may be imposed, government must offer a fair, speedy, and public trial. These are known as due process protections.

3. The protection against the assumption of power by the federal government. Those powers not given to the federal government through our Constitution remain with the states and the people.

The protections outlined in the Bill of Rights, along with the subsequent amendments, are summarized below.

The **1st Amendment** protects the people's right to practice religion, to speak freely, to assemble, to petition the government for the redress of any grievances, and freedom of the press. It also forbids the government from establishing a state-run religion.

The **2nd Amendment** protects the individual's right to keep and bear arms.

The **3rd Amendment** guarantees that the government cannot force homeowners to give members of the military room and board during war time or peace time.

The **4th Amendment** protects the people from the government improperly searching or seizing property or people, without a valid warrant based on probable cause. Exceptions to the warrant requirement do exist.

The **5th Amendment** protects people from being held for committing a crime unless they are properly indicted, that they may not be tried twice for the same crime, that they may not be forced to testify against themselves, and property may not be taken without just compensation. It also secures due process protections.

The **6th Amendment** guarantees a fair, public, and speedy trial, an impartial jury, along with the right to confront accusers, compel witnesses to testify in one's own defense, and to have a lawyer.

The **7th Amendment** guarantees a jury trial in civil court cases.

The **8th Amendment** prohibits the requirement of excessive bail, the imposition of excessive fines, or the infliction of cruel and unusual punishment.

The **9th Amendment** is simply a statement that other rights aside from those listed may exist. Simply because certain rights are not listed in the Constitution does not mean they do not exist. Instead, inherent liberties must be protected and cannot be infringed upon.

The **10th Amendment** states that any power not granted to the federal government belongs to the states or to the people.

The **11th Amendment** more clearly defines the original jurisdiction of the Supreme Court concerning a suit brought against a state by a citizen of another state. As a general proposition, states cannot be sued without their consent.

The **12th Amendment** redefines how the President and Vice-President are chosen by the Electoral College, making the two positions cooperative. It also ensures that anyone who becomes Vice-President must be eligible to become President.

The **13th Amendment** abolishes slavery or involuntary servitude in the United States.

The **14th Amendment** ensures that all citizens of all states enjoy not only rights on the federal level, but on the state level as well. The privileges and immunities, due process, and equal protection clauses all enhance the protections of the people at the state level. This amendment eliminated the counting of slaves as three-fifths of other persons as was originally set forth in Article I, Section 2. It ensures that the United States would not pay the debts of the rebellious states of the Civil War. It also had several measures designed to ensure the loyalty of legislators who participated on the Confederate side of the Civil War.

The **15th Amendment** ensures that race cannot be used as a criterion for voting.

The **16th Amendment** authorizes the United States to collect income tax without regard to the population of the states.

The **17th Amendment** shifts the choosing of senators from the state legislatures to the people of the states.

The **18th Amendment** abolished the sale or manufacture of alcohol in the United States. This amendment was later repealed by the 21st Amendment.

The **19th Amendment** ensures that gender cannot be used as a criterion for voting.

The **20th Amendment** set new start dates for the terms of the Congress and the President and clarifies how the deaths of presidents would be handled.

The **21st Amendment** repealed the 18th Amendment.

The **22nd Amendment** set a limit on the number of times a President could be elected: two four-year terms. It has one exception for a Vice-President who assumes the presidency after the death or removal of the President, establishing the maximum term of any president to 10 years.

The **23rd Amendment** grants the District of Columbia (Washington D.C.) the authorization to join the Electoral College with three electors for purposes of presidential elections.

The **24th Amendment** ensures that no tax could be charged to vote for any federal office.

The **25th Amendment** clarifies even further the line of succession to the presidency and establishes rules for a President who becomes unable to perform his duties while in office.

The **26th Amendment** ensures that any person who is at least 18 years old may vote.

The **27th Amendment** requires that any law that increases the pay of legislators may not take effect until after an election.

Lesson

1. Memorize the protections outlined in the various amendments. For example, come up with an acronym like SARPP to make it easier to commit the First Amendment to memory.
    a. **S**peech
    b. **A**ssembly
    c. **R**eligion
    d. **P**ress
    e. **P**etition the government for redress of grievances

2. Here is a helpful diagram to assist you in memorizing the amendments.

Amendment	Description
1st	Speech, assembly, religion, press, petition
2nd	Arms
3rd	Housing soldiers
4th	Search and seizure
5th	Rights of the accused
6th	Trial rights
7th	Jury trial in civil cases
8th	Punishment and Bail
9th	Rights retained by the people
10th	Powers to govern reserved to the states and the people
11th	Suits against the states
12th	Election of President and Vice President
13th	Abolition of Slavery
14th	Rights of citizenship
15th	Voting rights (all races protected)
16th	Income tax
17th	Election of senators
18th	Ban of alcohol
19th	Voting rights protected (men and women protected)
20th	Terms of office
21st	Repeal of the Eighteenth Amendment
22nd	Limit on presidential terms (Two terms)
23rd	Presidential electoral votes for Washington, DC
24th	Ban on poll taxes
25th	Presidential succession
26th	Voting age (Eighteen years old)
27th	Congressional compensation

Discussion Questions

1. When it comes to the need for the Bill of Rights, do you agree with James Madison or George Mason? If our liberties are inherent, why is there a need for the Bill of Rights?

2. Where do liberties such as speech come from? From the government, Constitution, the consent of the governed, or our "Creator"? Discuss the philosophical differences that emanate from these different answers.

3. What is the difference between the right of free speech, assembly, and property and the right to a fair, public, and speedy trial? (Hint: The former protects an inherent liberty of all human beings. The latter protects us from government as they seek to punish people for violating the rights of others (theft, murder, etc.) by ensuring due process protections.)

4. What is the most important liberty that, if lost, would potentially mean the demise of all other liberties?

5. Read the First Amendment. Does the text of the First Amendment allow a person to say anything that they want without consequence? What are the limitations on our various liberties?

6. Are the rights listed in the Bill of Rights individual or collective rights? Explain.

7. When the Constitution was ratified, it was primarily applicable only to the federal government. However, the Fourteenth Amendment initiated a change that ensured that state governments could not infringe on those protections outlined in the First Amendment, for example. Do you agree with this expansive application of the Constitution?

Chapter 24
American Exceptionalism

"The position of the American is...quite exceptional, and it may be believed that no democratic people will ever be placed in a similar one."
~Alexis de Tocqueville

You have certainly heard the phrase "American exceptionalism," but what does that mean? First, American exceptionalism is not based on some sort of nationalistic pride or a geographic region. America is exceptional for reasons far greater than location. American exceptionalism has much more to do with results produced by a government established to protect the people's liberty first and foremost.

Some people may identify the ills of a country and conclude that "greatness" or a superior system could not possibly be a reality. However, exceptionalim speaks to a cumulative, qualitative difference created in a society produced through opportunity protected by the rule of law.

It is imperative to note that America has constantly experienced an upward spiral towards more liberty with a few bumps along the way that had to be ironed out and are still being ironed out. How America has dealt with those obstacles is a reflection of her overarching values.

We could create an expansive list explaining why America is exceptional or different. No such list could be all-inclusive or would truly do America justice. However, some factors that must be considered in any such discussion are as follows:

America *is* exceptional because she was founded on a creed that all men are born free. In other words, our country was founded on the very idea of freedom and the source of that freedom, namely the "Creator," as noted in the Declaration of Independence. No other country was formed with the beginning proposition that people are inherently free. American government was established around this revolutionary idea.

America *is* exceptional because the ideal of equal treatment under the law is more than words on a piece of paper. They are words that many Americans have made the ultimate sacrifice to defend. Equality for all before the law, rather than mere professional status or affiliation, is essential to the freedom experiment.

America *is* exceptional because we can say and believe whatever we wish even if others disagree. Not only does it not matter if others disagree, in America it does not matter if the majority disagree. The marketplace of ideas has found a safe haven here in America.

America *is* exceptional because we drafted the world's first constitution that would carry the force of law and would be the model for many nations to follow. Today, it is the world's oldest constitution and for good reasons: separation of authority, division of power, popular sovereignty, a republican form of government, and the freedom ideal, to name only a few.

America *is* exceptional because we embrace innovation. We have 5% of the world's population, yet we consistently produce 25% of the world's wealth. Why? Is it mere happenstance or coincidence? Surely not. It is fundamentally because our Constitution protects the fruits of our labors and protects our right to acquire, possess, enjoy, and dispose of our property as we wish. When people have the opportunity to own their labor, prosperity results.

America *is* exceptional. People all over the world risk their lives to come to America. Indeed, those who risk their lives and who build makeshift boats to leave places like Haiti for a better life do not head to places like Jamaica, Cuba, the Island of Turk and Caicos, or even the Bahamas. Instead, they risk everything to come to America. Why? Do they look to America's infrastructure, what she protects, or what she promotes? Is it that America has a convenience store on every corner or because Bingo nights are en vogue? Or is it because we don't just talk about freedom, we actually strive to achieve that ideal?

America *is* exceptional because of our ingenuity, which is reflected by the fact that year after year Americans register more patents than anywhere else in the world. We simply create more, invent more, and produce more than any other country.

America *is* exceptional because of wealth-building opportunities that are protected by our Constitution. More millionaires are found in America than anywhere else on the planet.

America *is* exceptional because we enjoy true liberty—the freedom to speak, to assemble, to worship, to defend ourselves, to be left alone, acquire property, etc., which has been largely protected throughout America's history. And government cannot deprive a person of those liberties, without due process of law. Those due process protections are the lynchpin of the great American experiement.

America *is* exceptional because of the men and women in our military, who have vigorously defended American liberty from the beginning. Like those who have served and continue to serve in our military, are you prepared to pledge your life, your fortune, and your sacred honor?

The foregoing is just a sampling of the results produced by an industrious people protected by the rule of law that revolves around the inherent nature of liberty. Today is the day to celebrate freedom, and that celebration should revolve around American exceptionalism. What will you do to restore the vigor of America's exceptionalism?

Lesson

1. Review the U.S. Constitution and identify components of the document that have brought about exceptional

results in America. For example, look at the number of inventions that have come from the minds of Americans. Article I, Section 8 of the Constitution protects the ideas and creations of the individual, thus providing motivation for innovation. What are some additional examples?

2. Debate: Many people confuse American exceptionalism with the idea that Americans are "better." Instead, exceptionalism speaks to results produced as a result of freedoms that are afforded and protected. As you review the list above, debate how these results were produced. Did they indeed have something to do with our founding document or were there other contributing factors?

3. Illustration: Pull up two pictures, one of a mansion or beautiful building and one of a building that has a precarious structure. Identify that the more majestic building has promise because of its solid foundation, while the other lacks structural integrity. Emphasize that great results start with a solid foundation. America and her charters of freedom (Declaration of Independence and the Constitution) are the basis of the solid foundation that have produced stellar results that revolve around freedom.

Discussion Questions

1. What is American exceptionalism and what makes America exceptional?

2. Are those things that make America unique under attack? List some examples. What is the solution to preserving those principles?

3. Does American exceptionalism have anything to do with geographic location or nationalistic pride? Why or why not?

4. Consider the following quote: "The Constitution was not the founders gift to America. It was God's gift to the world." What are your thoughts about this quote as it relates to American exceptionalism?

Chapter 25
Defending the U.S. Constitution

"I know no safe depository of the ultimate powers of the society but the people themselves; and if we think them not enlightened enough to exercise their control with a wholesome discretion, the remedy is not to take it from them but to inform their discretion by education. This is the true corrective of abuses of Constitutional power."
~Thomas Jefferson

We often talk about freedom, but, sadly, many speak of defending the Constitution only as it relates to defending those principles that they believe in. For example, many defend the freedom of speech insofar as it pertains to speech that they agree with. Others claim to believe in the freedom of religion insofar as the religious practice in question conforms to their personal belief system. There is certainly a difference between promoting the values one embraces and using the force of law to secure an individual agenda. The former is a part of the American experiment. The latter jeopardizes freedom.

We cannot defend what we don't understand, and our Constitution cannot defend itself. Our charter of freedom is a mere piece of parchment that is only given teeth by the people who elect leaders who are restrained by the document. The Constitution is like a trap that stops tyrannical impulses. However, the trap is only effective if the people engage the trap to begin with. If we do not engage the trap, those with power ultimately have no limitations. Their actions simply hinge on the whims of the people, which are almost always selfish in nature.

If you are reading this book, you probably already agree that defending the Constitution is of paramount importance. As a result, the debate becomes what a person can do to defend the

Constitution, not whether the Constitution should be defended.

Getting the people to recognize the importance of the Constitution and the overarching principles of freedom that it protects is a cultural issue. As a people, we disregard the Constitution because we have "bought in" to the idea that the Constitution is not relevant and that those who lead have sincere motives that, more often than not, have the best interest of the people in mind. To change this historically inaccurate perception, we must be a voice for the rational defense of a ruling document that maximizes freedom and minimizes tyranny.

As we move forward defending the Constitution, recognize that no one person or organization is the answer. We the people are the answer. Each of us has been given certain talents that can assist in "taking the culture back." Whether we are a multi-millionaire who owns a radio station, a middle class worker who leads a community group, a stay-at-home mother who cares for a home full of children, or a struggling American trying to make ends meet, we all can play a role.

Think about this: What makes you tick? What do you enjoy doing? Do you enjoy speaking or stuffing envelopes? Are you good at organizing events or do you prefer to help non-profit organizations execute a plan? Are you efficient at social media or do you write well? There is room for everyone under the tent of freedom, and there is a need for everyone with their talents and passion to step forward.

There is an unending list of things that we can do. Let's examine the tip of the iceberg and consider what you can do to further the cause.

Understand the Message

1. Spend fifteen minutes a day studying a freedom principle. Seek out books that outline and educate on the essential ingredients of a free society.

2. Spend at least one hour per day listening to talk radio or TV commentary and reading the newspaper. We must stay on top of the issues of the day.

Social Media

1. Set up a social media account.

2. Engage in a discussion about the issues of the day. Give one patriotic thought per day.

Pledge Your Fortune

1. Contribute to organizations that move the liberty message across the country. They represent the focal point—the spearhead—of real change.

2. Support those radio and TV talk show hosts who are doing what is necessary to be a persuasive voice for less government and more freedom.

Expose America to the Right Ideas

1. Fly the American flag and encourage others to do the same.

2. Gather with your family, neighbors, and friends once monthly for "Freedom Night" or "Constitution Night."

Churches

1. Contact your local pastors, preachers, and other leaders. Invite them to set up a separate meeting to discuss the inspired nature of our Constitution with their congregation.

Schools

1. Contact your local school teachers, principals, and superintendents about putting on a presentation for their students about the Constitution.

Young People

1. Support our young people who are attempting to become involved and have their voice heard.

2. Create an environment that our young people find appealing. In order to change the culture, we must create something the culture will adopt through utlizing various attractive mediums.

Leadership

1. Become involved as a precinct committeeman in your legislative district in your state.

2. Become involved in your grassroots leadership core.

3. Think outside the box. As a leader, put together events and hold exciting meetings that will help build our audience and the overall movement.

Political Action

1. Send letters to both local and federal congressmen enumerating your concerns.

2. Get involved in local politics, including your state legislature, city council, and school boards. Know your representatives by name and participate in meetings and debates.

3. Run for political office.

Media

1. Send letters to the editor. Let your voice be heard!

2. Call and email radio hosts and TV anchors discussing your opinion on a current issue.

Grassroots Meetings

1. Get involved in grassroots organizations. Help to create meetings that are truly "outside the box." Move away from panel discussions on a regular basis. People learn in different ways and having someone speak from behind a microphone is simply one of many ways. Entertain! Educate! Empower!

Get involved. Encourage those around you. Be a beacon of hope. Recognize that restoration takes time and will happen one heart, one mind, one conversation at a time.

Lesson

1. Focus on doing one of the above suggestions every week. Discuss with your family and friends what you will do and commit to doing it.

2. Create a flyer about your love for America and pass them out throughout your neighborhood.

3. Now that you have completed this book, consider how you will call a meeting with extended family members, neighbors, and friends. Discuss a plan to begin engaging with others about the principles and lessons outlined in this book. Contemplate how you can set up weekly and/or monthly meetings.

4. At this point, you have proceeded through the entire Constitution. Let's engage in a challenge to amplify our knowledge. The following game will assist the participants in their understanding of our charters of freedom. (This game was a part of the 2010 Congress in the Classroom® competition.)

The Power Game—Checks and Balances in the Constitution:

a. Divide the class into three groups representing the executive, legislative, and judicial branches of government. Each student should have a copy of the Constitution with them.

b. In each round, the teacher will give each branch of government an opportunity for an unconstitutional "Power Grab." The remaining two groups have two minutes to find proof that the power grab is unconstitutional using the Constitution (amendments included) by article, section, and clause.

c. When a person thinks he has found the appropriate check he yells "check." He must be prepared to respond with the answer immediately. If wrong, others may try to block the grab for power within the two minutes, alternating between branches until the two minutes are gone or the answer is correct.

d. When checked correctly, the branch receives 10 points. If no one gets the correct answer, the branch-grabbing power gets 5 points. There is no penalty for wrong answers.

e. A round is a question for each branch, i.e., three questions in total.

Power Grabs by Round:

a. Round One
   1. Executive: The President decides to run for a third term. (Check: Amendment 22).
   2. Congress: Congress passes a law taking 10% of the value on lumber being exported. (Check: Article I, Section 9, Paragraph 5)
   3. Courts: The Court rules that the government may not issue patents because of the need for technological advance. (Check: Article I, Section 8, Paragraph 8)

b. Round Two
   1. Executive: The President declares war on China. (Check: Article I, Section 8, Paragraph 11)
   2. Congress: Congress passes a law that people from Washington may not drive cars in Oregon because of pollution. (Check: Article IV, Section 2, Paragraph 1)
   3. Courts: Since Washington, D.C. is not in any state, residents there may not vote in national elections. (Check: Amendment 23)

c. Round Three
   1. Executive: The President appoints John Smith to Senator Adams' seat when he resigns due to a personal scandal. (Check: Article I, Section 3, Paragraph 2)

2. Congress: Congress impeaches the President because he pardons a soldier. The Republican Congress uses their anger to retaliate. (Check: Article II, Section 4)

3. Courts: The Court rules that because of our large national debt, the U.S. can no longer borrow money. (Check: Article I, Section 8, Paragraph 2)

d. Round Four

1. President: To fight terrorism, anyone found guilty of hijacking will be punished by having their fingernails ripped off. (Check: Amendment 8)

2. Congress: Congress decides that beards are illegal. Anyone who wore one in the last year must pay a $100 fine. (Check: Article I, Section 9, Paragraph 3)

3. Courts: The Court decides that religion and politics don't mix. Therefore, no government official is required to take an oath of office. (Check: Article II, Section 1, Paragraph 8 or Article VI, Section 3)

e. Round Five

1. President: The President decides that Congress will meet in regular session on December 15 of each year. (Check: Amendment 20, Section 2)

2. Congress: Congress decides to impeach the President with the President Pro-Tempore of the Senate presiding. (Check: Article I, Section 3, Paragraph 6)

3. Courts: The ambassador to Spain is brought home and tried in a New York court for crimes. (Check: Article III, Section 2, Paragraph 1)

f. Round Six

1. President: The President orders that a mass murderer be sent back to Washington from Oregon. (Check: Article IV, Section 2, Paragraph 2)

2. Congress: A House member dies, the House takes four days off to mourn, but the Senate says they can only have two days off. (Check: Article I, Section 5, Paragraph 4)

3. Courts: The Court rules that the heads of departments may no longer make appointments of inferior officers, but only the President may do so. (Check: Article II, Section 2, Paragraph 2)

g. Round Seven

1. President: A Hollywood maniac comes to town and cuts off the heads of all parking meters. The President pardons her after she is convicted of criminal damage. (Check: Article II, Section 2, Paragraph 1)

2. Congress: Congress passes a law naming fifteen university students guilty of crimes against the government and orders them expelled from school. (Check: Article I, Section 9, Paragraph 3)

3. Courts: A male teacher sues over sexual discrimination by taking the case directly to the Supreme Court. (Check: Article III, Section 2, Paragraph 2)

h. Round Eight

1. President: Your land is in the way of a proposed plan to build a federal highway, so the President takes your land without compensation. (Check: Amendment 5)

2. Congress: Congress passes a law that says you can sue your state in federal court. (Check: Amendment 11)

3. Courts: The Court rules that income tax is illegal, and you don't have to pay. (Check: Amendment 16)

i. Round Nine

1. President: The President orders that since all citizens over 18 want to vote for the President, they may do so by popular vote. (Check: Amendment 26)

2. Congress: Congress decides because of the contributions of Pete Rose in baseball, they will honor him with the title, "Sir Pete Rose." (Check: Article 1, Section 10, Paragraph 1)

3. Courts: The Court rules that because of the difficulty of finding honest, law-abiding people, they will allow Senator Jane Doe to be Secretary of Interior. (Check: Article I, Section 6, Paragraph 2)

j. Round Ten
   1. President: The President, concerned about drug violations in the state of Washington, allows the Governor and Attorney General to suspend democracy for a period of one month. (Check: Article IV, Section 4)
   2. Congress: Congress decides to create a federal law allowing the President to be elected to only one term of six years. (Check: Amendment 22)
   3. Courts: The Courts find Suspect A guilty of treason on the basis of the testimony of Witness B alone. (Check: Article III, Section 3, Paragraph 1)

Discussion Questions

1. What talents do you have that can help move the message of freedom in your family, in your community, and throughout the country? In a group discussion, each person should take the time to identify the talents of everyone else in the group.

2. What issues are you most concerned about in America today or even throughout the world? What can you do about them?

3. What things would you add to the list above as we focus on restoring the foundational principles of America?

Afterword
Freedom Takes Commitment

Freedom and its preservation is a project that knows no intermission or rest. Either we will actively defend it or it will disappear at the hands of our neglect. Each generation has relied on the previous generation to pass them the torch of what is ultimately their birthright. Sadly, few generations have ever passed on that gift. As a result, few people have ever experienced what it is like to be free. For the few who have experienced it, it has been a struggle because apathy is a pervasive human condition. You can change that.

We must be the generation who preserves liberty and who passes it on to our children and grandchildren. As John Adams said, "I must study politics and war that my sons may have liberty to study mathematics and philosophy."

What can we do as a people to steer this ship to the promised land? Consider just a few of these steps.

1. Know and understand the Constitution.

2. Recognize and live out the principles of liberty.

3. Become civically active. Participate in the politics of your community.

4. Become active with your family, friends, and neighbors and teach within your sphere of influence.

5. Elect individuals who understand the Constitution and the accomp.anying principles of liberty.

6. Hold your representatives accountable.

7. Engage in the contest of ideas each day of your life. Liberty and tyranny are the two contestants on the field. Defend liberty by becoming educated, involved, and informed.

Daniel Webster perhaps said it best, and we would be wise

to heed his counsel. "Hold on, my friends, to the Constitution and to the Republic for which it stands. Miracles do not cluster and what has happened once in 6,000 years, may not happen again. Hold on to the Constitution, for if the American Constitution should fail, there will be anarchy throughout the world."

Together we can defend liberty. We can reignite the spirit of our founders. We can restore America and the matchless opportunities she has provided to the human race here and throughout the world. The future is counting on our efforts.

We started our journey by asking the quesitons "What is freedom?" and "Is it for you?" Hopefully, you've concluded that there are fewer causes more important than freedom, for it defines and enhances our lives, our associations, our productivity, and our purpose. Great things are accomplished when a society is focused on defending freedom as a first priority.

Imagine your grandchildren standing in front of class full of their colleagues decades from now reporting on our generation. What will they say about your efforts? What condition will they live in? Will they look at you with honor and recognize that you fought to maintain their liberty?

Libery is not just for you. It is for all of us, regardless of our geographic region. Stand up, be counted, and have the courage to defend what so few are willing to defend. After all, this is our birthright to preserve!

The Declaration of Independence

IN CONGRESS, July 4, 1776.

The unanimous Declaration of the thirteen united States of America,

When in the Course of human events, it becomes necessary for one people to dissolve the political bands which have connected them with another, and to assume among the powers of the earth, the separate and equal station to which the Laws of Nature and of Nature's God entitle them, a decent respect to the opinions of mankind requires that they should declare the causes which impel them to the separation.

We hold these truths to be self-evident, that all men are created equal, that they are endowed by their Creator with certain unalienable Rights, that among these are Life, Liberty and the pursuit of Happiness.—That to secure these rights, Governments are instituted among Men, deriving their just powers from the consent of the governed, —That whenever any Form of Government becomes destructive of these ends, it is the Right of the People to alter or to abolish it, and to institute new Government, laying its foundation on such principles and organizing its powers in such form, as to them shall seem most likely to effect their Safety and Happiness. Prudence, indeed, will dictate that Governments long established should not be changed for light and transient causes; and accordingly all experience hath shewn, that mankind are more disposed to suffer, while evils are sufferable, than to right themselves by abolishing the forms to which they are accustomed. But when a long train of abuses and usurpations, pursuing invariably the same Object evinces a design to reduce them under absolute Despotism, it is their right, it is their duty, to throw off such Government, and to provide new Guards for their future security.—

Such has been the patient sufferance of these Colonies; and such is now the necessity which constrains them to alter their former Systems of Government. The history of the present King of Great Britain is a history of repeated injuries and usurpations, all having in direct object the establishment of an absolute Tyranny over these States. To prove this, let Facts be submitted to a candid world.

He has refused his Assent to Laws, the most wholesome and necessary for the public good.

He has forbidden his Governors to pass Laws of immediate and pressing importance, unless suspended in their operation till his Assent should be obtained; and when so suspended, he has utterly neglected to attend to them.

He has refused to pass other Laws for the accommodation of large districts of people, unless those people would relinquish the right of Representation in the Legislature, a right inestimable to them and formidable to tyrants only.

He has called together legislative bodies at places unusual, uncomfortable, and distant from the depository of their public Records, for the sole purpose of fatiguing them into compliance with his measures.

He has dissolved Representative Houses repeatedly, for opposing with manly firmness his invasions on the rights of the people.

He has refused for a long time, after such dissolutions, to cause others to be elected; whereby the Legislative powers, incapable of Annihilation, have returned to the People at large for their exercise; the State remaining in the mean time exposed to all the dangers of invasion from without, and convulsions within.

He has endeavoured to prevent the population of these States; for that purpose obstructing the Laws for Naturalization of Foreigners; refusing to pass others to encourage their migrations hither, and raising the conditions of new Appropriations of Lands.

He has obstructed the Administration of Justice, by refusing his Assent to Laws for establishing Judiciary powers.

He has made Judges dependent on his Will alone, for the tenure of their offices, and the amount and payment of their salaries.

He has erected a multitude of New Offices, and sent hither swarms of Officers to harrass our people, and eat out their substance.

He has kept among us, in times of peace, Standing Armies without the Consent of our legislatures.

He has affected to render the Military independent of and superior to the Civil power.

He has combined with others to subject us to a jurisdiction foreign to our constitution, and unacknowledged by our laws; giving his Assent to their Acts of pretended Legislation:

For Quartering large bodies of armed troops among us:

For protecting them, by a mock Trial, from punishment for any Murders which they should commit on the Inhabitants of these States:

For cutting off our Trade with all parts of the world:

For imposing Taxes on us without our Consent:

For depriving us in many cases, of the benefits of Trial by Jury:

For transporting us beyond Seas to be tried for pretended offences

For abolishing the free System of English Laws in a neighbouring Province, establishing therein an Arbitrary government, and enlarging its Boundaries so as to render it at once an example and fit instrument for introducing the same absolute rule into these Colonies:

For taking away our Charters, abolishing our most valuable Laws, and altering fundamentally the Forms of our Governments:

For suspending our own Legislatures, and declaring themselves invested with power to legislate for us in all cases whatsoever.

He has abdicated Government here, by declaring us out of his Protection and waging War against us.

He has plundered our seas, ravaged our Coasts, burnt our towns, and destroyed the lives of our people.

He is at this time transporting large Armies of foreign Mercenaries to compleat the works of death, desolation and tyranny, already begun with circumstances of Cruelty & perfidy scarcely paralleled in the most barbarous ages, and totally unworthy the Head of a civilized nation.

He has constrained our fellow Citizens taken Captive on the high Seas to bear Arms against their Country, to become the executioners of their friends and Brethren, or to fall themselves by their Hands.

He has excited domestic insurrections amongst us, and has endeavoured to bring on the inhabitants of our frontiers, the merciless Indian Savages, whose known rule of warfare, is an undistinguished destruction of all ages, sexes and conditions.

In every stage of these Oppressions We have Petitioned for Redress in the most humble terms: Our repeated Petitions have been answered only by repeated injury. A Prince whose character is thus marked by every act which may define a Tyrant, is unfit to be the ruler of a free people.

Nor have We been wanting in attentions to our Brittish brethren. We have warned them from time to time of attempts by their legislature to extend an unwarrantable jurisdiction over us. We have reminded them of the circumstances of our emigration and settlement here. We have appealed to their native justice and magnanimity, and we have conjured them by the ties of our common kindred to disavow these usurpations, which, would inevitably interrupt our connections and correspondence. They too have been deaf to the voice of justice and of consanguinity. We must, therefore, acquiesce in the necessity, which denounces our Separation, and hold them, as we hold the rest of mankind, Enemies in War, in Peace Friends.

We, therefore, the Representatives of the united States of America, in General Congress, Assembled, appealing to the Supreme Judge of the world for the rectitude of our intentions, do, in the Name, and by Authority of the good People of these Colonies, solemnly publish and declare, That these United Colonies are, and of Right ought to be Free and Independent States; that they are Absolved from all Allegiance to the British Crown, and that all political connection between them and the State of Great Britain, is and ought to be totally dissolved; and that as Free and Independent States, they have full Power to levy War, conclude Peace, contract Alliances, establish Commerce, and to do all other Acts and Things which Independent States may of right do. And for the support of this Declaration, with a firm reliance on the protection of divine Providence, we mutually pledge to each other our Lives, our Fortunes and our sacred Honor.

The 56 signatures on the Declaration of Independence appear below:

Georgia:
Button Gwinnett
Lyman Hall
George Walton

North Carolina:
William Hooper
Joseph Hewes
John Penn

South Carolina:
Edward Rutledge
Thomas Heyward, Jr.
Thomas Lynch, Jr.
Arthur Middleton

Massachusetts:
John Hancock

Maryland:
Samuel Chase
William Paca
Thomas Stone
Charles Carroll of Carrollton

Virginia:
George Wythe
Richard Henry Lee
Thomas Jefferson
Benjamin Harrison
Thomas Nelson, Jr.
Francis Lightfoot Lee
Carter Braxton

Pennsylvania:
Robert Morris
Benjamin Rush
Benjamin Franklin
John Morton
George Clymer
James Smith
George Taylor
James Wilson
George Ross

Delaware:
Caesar Rodney
George Read
Thomas McKean

New York:
William Floyd
Philip Livingston
Francis Lewis
Lewis Morris

New Jersey:
Richard Stockton
John Witherspoon
Francis Hopkinson
John Hart
Abraham Clark

New Hampshire:
Josiah Bartlett
William Whipple

Massachusetts:
Samuel Adams
John Adams
Robert Treat Paine
Elbridge Gerry

Rhode Island:
Stephen Hopkins
William Ellery

Connecticut:
Roger Sherman
Samuel Huntington
William Williams
Oliver Wolcott

New Hampshire:
Matthew Thornton

The Constitution of the United States

Note: *The following text is a transcription of the Constitution in its **original** form.*
Items that are underlined have since been amended or superseded.

We the People of the United States, in Order to form a more perfect Union, establish Justice, insure domestic Tranquility, provide for the common defence, promote the general Welfare, and secure the Blessings of Liberty to ourselves and our Posterity, do ordain and establish this Constitution for the United States of America.

Article. I.

Section. 1.

All legislative Powers herein granted shall be vested in a Congress of the United States, which shall consist of a Senate and House of Representatives.

Section. 2.

The House of Representatives shall be composed of Members chosen every second Year by the People of the several States, and the Electors in each State shall have the Qualifications requisite for Electors of the most numerous Branch of the State Legislature.

No Person shall be a Representative who shall not have attained to the Age of twenty five Years, and been seven Years a Citizen of the United States, and who shall not, when elected, be an Inhabitant of that State in which he shall be chosen.

Representatives and direct Taxes shall be apportioned among the several States which may be included within this

Union, according to their respective Numbers, which shall be determined by adding to the whole Number of free Persons, including those bound to Service for a Term of Years, and excluding Indians not taxed, three fifths of all other Persons. The actual Enumeration shall be made within three Years after the first Meeting of the Congress of the United States, and within every subsequent Term of ten Years, in such Manner as they shall by Law direct. The Number of Representatives shall not exceed one for every thirty Thousand, but each State shall have at Least one Representative; and until such enumeration shall be made, the State of New Hampshire shall be entitled to chuse three, Massachusetts eight, Rhode-Island and Providence Plantations one, Connecticut five, New-York six, New Jersey four, Pennsylvania eight, Delaware one, Maryland six, Virginia ten, North Carolina five, South Carolina five, and Georgia three.

When vacancies happen in the Representation from any State, the Executive Authority thereof shall issue Writs of Election to fill such Vacancies.

The House of Representatives shall chuse their Speaker and other Officers; and shall have the sole Power of Impeachment.

Section. 3.

The Senate of the United States shall be composed of two Senators from each State, chosen by the Legislature thereof for six Years; and each Senator shall have one Vote.

Immediately after they shall be assembled in Consequence of the first Election, they shall be divided as equally as may be into three Classes. The Seats of the Senators of the first Class shall be vacated at the Expiration of the second Year, of the second Class at the Expiration of the fourth Year, and of the third Class at the Expiration of the sixth Year, so that one third may be chosen every second Year; and if Vacancies happen by Resignation, or otherwise, during the Recess of the Legislature of any State, the Executive thereof may make temporary Appointments until the next Meeting of the Legislature, which shall then fill such Vacancies.

No Person shall be a Senator who shall not have attained to the Age of thirty Years, and been nine Years a Citizen of the United States, and who shall not, when elected, be an Inhabitant of that State for which he shall be chosen.

The Vice President of the United States shall be President of the Senate, but shall have no Vote, unless they be equally divided.

The Senate shall chuse their other Officers, and also a President pro tempore, in the Absence of the Vice President, or when he shall exercise the Office of President of the United States.

The Senate shall have the sole Power to try all Impeachments. When sitting for that Purpose, they shall be on Oath or Affirmation. When the President of the United States is tried, the Chief Justice shall preside: And no Person shall be convicted without the Concurrence of two thirds of the Members present.

Judgment in Cases of Impeachment shall not extend further than to removal from Office, and disqualification to hold and enjoy any Office of honor, Trust or Profit under the United States: but the Party convicted shall nevertheless be liable and subject to Indictment, Trial, Judgment and Punishment, according to Law.

Section. 4.

The Times, Places and Manner of holding Elections for Senators and Representatives, shall be prescribed in each State by the Legislature thereof; but the Congress may at any time by Law make or alter such Regulations, except as to the Places of chusing Senators.

The Congress shall assemble at least once in every Year, and such Meeting shall be on the first Monday in December, unless they shall by Law appoint a different Day.

Section. 5.

Each House shall be the Judge of the Elections, Returns and Qualifications of its own Members, and a Majority of each shall constitute a Quorum to do Business; but a smaller Number may adjourn from day to day, and may be authorized to compel the Attendance of absent Members, in such Manner, and under such Penalties as each House may provide.

Each House may determine the Rules of its Proceedings, punish its Members for disorderly Behaviour, and, with the Concurrence of two thirds, expel a Member.

Each House shall keep a Journal of its Proceedings, and from time to time publish the same, excepting such Parts as may in their Judgment require Secrecy; and the Yeas and Nays of the Members of either House on any question shall, at the Desire of one fifth of those Present, be entered on the Journal.

Neither House, during the Session of Congress, shall, without the Consent of the other, adjourn for more than three days, nor to any other Place than that in which the two Houses shall be sitting.

Section. 6.

The Senators and Representatives shall receive a Compensation for their Services, to be ascertained by Law, and paid out of the Treasury of the United States. They shall in all Cases, except Treason, Felony and Breach of the Peace, be privileged from Arrest during their Attendance at the Session of their respective Houses, and in going to and returning from the same; and for any Speech or Debate in either House, they shall not be questioned in any other Place.

No Senator or Representative shall, during the Time for which he was elected, be appointed to any civil Office under the Authority of the United States, which shall have been created, or the Emoluments whereof shall have been encreased during such time; and no Person holding any Office under the United States, shall be a Member of either House during his Continuance in Office.

Section. 7.

All Bills for raising Revenue shall originate in the House of Representatives; but the Senate may propose or concur with Amendments as on other Bills.

Every Bill which shall have passed the House of Representatives and the Senate, shall, before it become a Law, be presented to the President of the United States: If he approve he shall sign it, but if not he shall return it, with his Objections to that House in which it shall have originated, who shall enter the Objections at large on their Journal, and proceed to reconsider it. If after such Reconsideration two thirds of that House shall agree to pass the Bill, it shall be sent, together with the Objections, to the other House, by which it shall likewise be reconsidered, and if approved by two thirds of that House, it shall become a Law. But in all such Cases the Votes of both Houses shall be determined by yeas and Nays, and the Names of the Persons voting for and against the Bill shall be entered on the Journal of each House respectively. If any Bill shall not be returned by the President within ten Days (Sundays excepted) after it shall have been presented to him, the Same shall be a Law, in like Manner as if he had signed it, unless the Congress by their Adjournment prevent its Return, in which Case it shall not be a Law.

Every Order, Resolution, or Vote to which the Concurrence of the Senate and House of Representatives may be necessary (except on a question of Adjournment) shall be presented to the President of the United States; and before the Same shall take Effect, shall be approved by him, or being disapproved by him, shall be repassed by two thirds of the Senate and House of Representatives, according to the Rules and Limitations prescribed in the Case of a Bill.

Section. 8.

The Congress shall have Power To lay and collect Taxes, Duties, Imposts and Excises, to pay the Debts and provide for the common Defence and general Welfare of the United States; but all Duties, Imposts and Excises shall be uniform throughout the United States;

To borrow Money on the credit of the United States;

To regulate Commerce with foreign Nations, and among the several States, and with the Indian Tribes;

To establish an uniform Rule of Naturalization, and uniform Laws on the subject of Bankruptcies throughout the United States;

To coin Money, regulate the Value thereof, and of foreign Coin, and fix the Standard of Weights and Measures;

To provide for the Punishment of counterfeiting the Securities and current Coin of the United States;

To establish Post Offices and post Roads;

To promote the Progress of Science and useful Arts, by securing for limited Times to Authors and Inventors the exclusive Right to their respective Writings and Discoveries;

To constitute Tribunals inferior to the supreme Court;

To define and punish Piracies and Felonies committed on the high Seas, and Offences against the Law of Nations;

To declare War, grant Letters of Marque and Reprisal, and make Rules concerning Captures on Land and Water;

To raise and support Armies, but no Appropriation of Money to that Use shall be for a longer Term than two Years;

To provide and maintain a Navy;

To make Rules for the Government and Regulation of the land and naval Forces;

To provide for calling forth the Militia to execute the Laws of the Union, suppress Insurrections and repel Invasions;

To provide for organizing, arming, and disciplining, the Militia, and for governing such Part of them as may be employed in the Service of the United States, reserving to the States respectively, the Appointment of the Officers, and the Authority of training the Militia according to the discipline prescribed by Congress;

To exercise exclusive Legislation in all Cases whatsoever, over such District (not exceeding ten Miles square) as may, by Cession of particular States, and the Acceptance of Congress, become the Seat of the Government of the United States, and to exercise like Authority over all Places purchased by the Consent of the Legislature of the State in which the Same shall be, for the Erection of Forts, Magazines, Arsenals, dock-Yards, and other needful Buildings;—And

To make all Laws which shall be necessary and proper for carrying into Execution the foregoing Powers, and all other Powers vested by this Constitution in the Government of the United States, or in any Department or Officer thereof.

Section. 9.

The Migration or Importation of such Persons as any of the States now existing shall think proper to admit, shall not be prohibited by the Congress prior to the Year one thousand eight hundred and eight, but a Tax or duty may be imposed on such Importation, not exceeding ten dollars for each Person.

The Privilege of the Writ of Habeas Corpus shall not be suspended, unless when in Cases of Rebellion or Invasion the public Safety may require it.

No Bill of Attainder or ex post facto Law shall be passed.

No Capitation, or other direct, Tax shall be laid, <u>unless in Proportion to the Census or enumeration herein before directed to be taken.</u>

No Tax or Duty shall be laid on Articles exported from any State.

No Preference shall be given by any Regulation of Commerce or Revenue to the Ports of one State over those of another; nor shall Vessels bound to, or from, one State, be obliged to enter, clear, or pay Duties in another.

No Money shall be drawn from the Treasury, but in Consequence of Appropriations made by Law; and a regular Statement and Account of the Receipts and Expenditures of all public Money shall be published from time to time.

No Title of Nobility shall be granted by the United States: And no Person holding any Office of Profit or Trust under them, shall, without the Consent of the Congress, accept of any present, Emolument, Office, or Title, of any kind whatever, from any King, Prince, or foreign State.

Section. 10.

No State shall enter into any Treaty, Alliance, or Confederation; grant Letters of Marque and Reprisal; coin Money; emit Bills of Credit; make any Thing but gold and silver Coin a Tender in Payment of Debts; pass any Bill of Attainder, ex post facto Law, or Law impairing the Obligation of Contracts, or grant any Title of Nobility.

No State shall, without the Consent of the Congress, lay any Imposts or Duties on Imports or Exports, except what may be absolutely necessary for executing it's inspection Laws: and the net Produce of all Duties and Imposts, laid by any State on Imports or Exports, shall be for the Use of the Treasury of the United States; and all such Laws shall be subject to the Revision and Controul of the Congress.

No State shall, without the Consent of Congress, lay any Duty of Tonnage, keep Troops, or Ships of War in time of Peace, enter into any Agreement or Compact with another State, or with a foreign Power, or engage in War, unless actually invaded, or in such imminent Danger as will not admit of delay.

Article. II.

Section. 1.

The executive Power shall be vested in a President of the United States of America. He shall hold his Office during the Term of four Years, and, together with the Vice President, chosen for the same Term, be elected, as follows:

Each State shall appoint, in such Manner as the Legislature thereof may direct, a Number of Electors, equal to the whole Number of Senators and Representatives to which the State may be entitled in the Congress: but no Senator or Representative, or Person holding an Office of Trust or Profit under the United States, shall be appointed an Elector.

The Electors shall meet in their respective States, and vote by Ballot for two Persons, of whom one at least shall not be an Inhabitant of the same State with themselves. And they shall make a List of all the Persons voted for, and of the Number of Votes for each; which List they shall sign and certify, and transmit sealed to the Seat of the Government of the United States, directed to the President of the Senate. The President of the Senate shall, in the Presence of the Senate and House of Representatives, open all the Certificates, and the Votes shall then be counted. The Person having the greatest Number of Votes shall be the President, if such Number be a Majority of the whole Number of Electors appointed; and if there be more than one who have such Majority, and have an equal Number of Votes, then the House of Representatives shall immediately chuse by Ballot one of them for President; and if no Person have a Majority, then from the five highest on the List the said House shall in like Manner chuse the President. But in chusing the President, the Votes shall be taken by States, the Representation from each State having one Vote; A quorum for this purpose shall consist of a Member or Members from two thirds of the States, and a Majority of all the States shall be necessary to a Choice. In every

Case, after the Choice of the President, the Person having the greatest Number of Votes of the Electors shall be the Vice President. But if there should remain two or more who have equal Votes, the Senate shall chuse from them by Ballot the Vice President.

The Congress may determine the Time of chusing the Electors, and the Day on which they shall give their Votes; which Day shall be the same throughout the United States.

No Person except a natural born Citizen, or a Citizen of the United States, at the time of the Adoption of this Constitution, shall be eligible to the Office of President; neither shall any Person be eligible to that Office who shall not have attained to the Age of thirty five Years, and been fourteen Years a Resident within the United States.

In Case of the Removal of the President from Office, or of his Death, Resignation, or Inability to discharge the Powers and Duties of the said Office, the Same shall devolve on the Vice President, and the Congress may by Law provide for the Case of Removal, Death, Resignation or Inability, both of the President and Vice President, declaring what Officer shall then act as President, and such Officer shall act accordingly, until the Disability be removed, or a President shall be elected.

The President shall, at stated Times, receive for his Services, a Compensation, which shall neither be increased nor diminished during the Period for which he shall have been elected, and he shall not receive within that Period any other Emolument from the United States, or any of them.

Before he enter on the Execution of his Office, he shall take the following Oath or Affirmation:—"I do solemnly swear (or affirm) that I will faithfully execute the Office of President of the United States, and will to the best of my Ability, preserve, protect and defend the Constitution of the United States."

Section. 2.

The President shall be Commander in Chief of the Army and Navy of the United States, and of the Militia of the several States, when called into the actual Service of the United States; he may require the Opinion, in writing, of the principal Officer in each of the executive Departments, upon any Subject relating to the Duties of their respective Offices, and he shall have Power to grant Reprieves and Pardons for Offences against the United States, except in Cases of Impeachment.

He shall have Power, by and with the Advice and Consent of the Senate, to make Treaties, provided two thirds of the Senators present concur; and he shall nominate, and by and with the Advice and Consent of the Senate, shall appoint Ambassadors, other public Ministers and Consuls, Judges of the supreme Court, and all other Officers of the United States, whose Appointments are not herein otherwise provided for, and which shall be established by Law: but the Congress may by Law vest the Appointment of such inferior Officers, as they think proper, in the President alone, in the Courts of Law, or in the Heads of Departments.

The President shall have Power to fill up all Vacancies that may happen during the Recess of the Senate, by granting Commissions which shall expire at the End of their next Session.

Section. 3.

He shall from time to time give to the Congress Information of the State of the Union, and recommend to their Consideration such Measures as he shall judge necessary and expedient; he may, on extraordinary Occasions, convene both Houses, or either of them, and in Case of Disagreement between them, with Respect to the Time of Adjournment, he may adjourn them to such Time as he shall think proper; he shall receive Ambassadors and other public Ministers; he shall take Care that the Laws be faithfully executed, and shall Commission all the Officers of the United States.

Section. 4.

The President, Vice President and all civil Officers of the United States, shall be removed from Office on Impeachment for, and Conviction of, Treason, Bribery, or other high Crimes and Misdemeanors.

Article III.

Section. 1.

The judicial Power of the United States shall be vested in one supreme Court, and in such inferior Courts as the Congress may from time to time ordain and establish. The Judges, both of the supreme and inferior Courts, shall hold their Offices during good Behaviour, and shall, at stated Times, receive for their Services a Compensation, which shall not be diminished during their Continuance in Office.

Section. 2.

The judicial Power shall extend to all Cases, in Law and Equity, arising under this Constitution, the Laws of the United States, and Treaties made, or which shall be made, under their Authority;—to all Cases affecting Ambassadors, other public Ministers and Consuls;—to all Cases of admiralty and maritime Jurisdiction;—to Controversies to which the United States shall be a Party;—to Controversies between two or more States;— between a State and Citizens of another State,—between Citizens of different States,—between Citizens of the same State claiming Lands under Grants of different States, and between a State, or the Citizens thereof, and foreign States, Citizens or Subjects.

In all Cases affecting Ambassadors, other public Ministers and Consuls, and those in which a State shall be Party, the supreme Court shall have original Jurisdiction. In all the other Cases before mentioned, the supreme Court shall have appellate Jurisdiction, both as to Law and Fact, with such Exceptions, and under such Regulations as the Congress shall make.

The Trial of all Crimes, except in Cases of Impeachment, shall be by Jury; and such Trial shall be held in the State where the said Crimes shall have been committed; but when not committed within any State, the Trial shall be at such Place or Places as the Congress may by Law have directed.

Section. 3.

Treason against the United States, shall consist only in levying War against them, or in adhering to their Enemies, giving them Aid and Comfort. No Person shall be convicted of Treason unless on the Testimony of two Witnesses to the same overt Act, or on Confession in open Court.

The Congress shall have Power to declare the Punishment of Treason, but no Attainder of Treason shall work Corruption of Blood, or Forfeiture except during the Life of the Person attainted.

Article. IV.

Section. 1.

Full Faith and Credit shall be given in each State to the public Acts, Records, and judicial Proceedings of every other State. And the Congress may by general Laws prescribe the Manner in which such Acts, Records and Proceedings shall be proved, and the Effect thereof.

Section. 2.

The Citizens of each State shall be entitled to all Privileges and Immunities of Citizens in the several States.

A Person charged in any State with Treason, Felony, or other Crime, who shall flee from Justice, and be found in another

State, shall on Demand of the executive Authority of the State from which he fled, be delivered up, to be removed to the State having Jurisdiction of the Crime.

No Person held to Service or Labour in one State, under the Laws thereof, escaping into another, shall, in Consequence of any Law or Regulation therein, be discharged from such Service or Labour, but shall be delivered up on Claim of the Party to whom such Service or Labour may be due.

Section. 3.

New States may be admitted by the Congress into this Union; but no new State shall be formed or erected within the Jurisdiction of any other State; nor any State be formed by the Junction of two or more States, or Parts of States, without the Consent of the Legislatures of the States concerned as well as of the Congress.

The Congress shall have Power to dispose of and make all needful Rules and Regulations respecting the Territory or other Property belonging to the United States; and nothing in this Constitution shall be so construed as to Prejudice any Claims of the United States, or of any particular State.

Section. 4.

The United States shall guarantee to every State in this Union a Republican Form of Government, and shall protect each of them against Invasion; and on Application of the Legislature, or of the Executive (when the Legislature cannot be convened), against domestic Violence.

Article. V.

The Congress, whenever two thirds of both Houses shall deem it necessary, shall propose Amendments to this Constitution, or, on the Application of the Legislatures of two thirds of the several States, shall call a Convention for proposing

Amendments, which, in either Case, shall be valid to all Intents and Purposes, as Part of this Constitution, when ratified by the Legislatures of three fourths of the several States, or by Conventions in three fourths thereof, as the one or the other Mode of Ratification may be proposed by the Congress; Provided that no Amendment which may be made prior to the Year One thousand eight hundred and eight shall in any Manner affect the first and fourth Clauses in the Ninth Section of the first Article; and that no State, without its Consent, shall be deprived of its equal Suffrage in the Senate.

Article. VI.

All Debts contracted and Engagements entered into, before the Adoption of this Constitution, shall be as valid against the United States under this Constitution, as under the Confederation.

This Constitution, and the Laws of the United States which shall be made in Pursuance thereof; and all Treaties made, or which shall be made, under the Authority of the United States, shall be the supreme Law of the Land; and the Judges in every State shall be bound thereby, any Thing in the Constitution or Laws of any State to the Contrary notwithstanding.

The Senators and Representatives before mentioned, and the Members of the several State Legislatures, and all executive and judicial Officers, both of the United States and of the several States, shall be bound by Oath or Affirmation, to support this Constitution; but no religious Test shall ever be required as a Qualification to any Office or public Trust under the United States.

Article. VII.

The Ratification of the Conventions of nine States, shall be sufficient for the Establishment of this Constitution between the States so ratifying the Same.

The Word, "the," being interlined between the seventh and eighth Lines of the first Page, the Word "Thirty" being partly written on an Erazure in the fifteenth Line of the first Page, The Words "is tried" being interlined between the thirty second and thirty third Lines of the first Page and the Word "the" being interlined between the forty third and forty fourth Lines of the second Page.

Attest William Jackson Secretary

done in Convention by the Unanimous Consent of the States present the Seventeenth Day of September in the Year of our Lord one thousand seven hundred and Eighty seven and of the Independance of the United States of America the Twelfth In witness whereof We have hereunto subscribed our Names,

G°. Washington
Presidt and deputy from Virginia

Delaware
Geo: Read
Gunning Bedford jun
John Dickinson
Richard Bassett
Jaco: Broom

Maryland
James McHenry
Dan of St Thos. Jenifer
Danl. Carroll

Virginia
John Blair
James Madison Jr.

North Carolina
Wm. Blount
Richd. Dobbs Spaight
Hu Williamson

South Carolina
J. Rutledge
Charles Cotesworth Pinckney
Charles Pinckney
Pierce Butler

Georgia
William Few
Abr Baldwin

New Hampshire
John Langdon
Nicholas Gilman

Massachusetts
Nathaniel Gorham
Rufus King

Connecticut
Wm. Saml. Johnson
Roger Sherman

New York
Alexander Hamilton

New Jersey
Wil: Livingston
David Brearley
Wm. Paterson
Jona: Dayton

Pennsylvania
B Franklin
Thomas Mifflin
Robt. Morris
Geo. Clymer
Thos. FitzSimons
Jared Ingersoll
James Wilson
Gouv Morris

Appendix C:
The Bill of Rights
and Subsequent Amendments

The Preamble to The Bill of Rights

Congress of the United States begun and held at the City of New-York, on Wednesday the fourth of March, one thousand seven hundred and eighty nine.

THE Conventions of a number of the States, having at the time of their adopting the Constitution, expressed a desire, in order to prevent misconstruction or abuse of its powers, that further declaratory and restrictive clauses should be added:And as extending the ground of public confidence in the Government, will best ensure the beneficent ends of its institution.

RESOLVED by the Senate and House of Representatives of the United States of America, in Congress assembled, two thirds of both Houses concurring, that the following Articles be proposed to the Legislatures of the several States, as ·amendments to the Constitution of the United States, all, or any of which Articles, when ratified by three fourths of the said Legislatures, to be valid to all intents and purposes, as part of the said Constitution; viz.

ARTICLES in addition to, and Amendment of the Constitution of the United States of America, proposed by Congress, and ratified by the Legislatures of the several States, pursuant to the fifth Article of the original Constitution.

Note:The following text is a transcription of the first ten amendments to the Constitution in their original form.These amendments were ratified December 15, 1791, and form what is known as the "Bill of Rights."

Amendment I

Congress shall make no law respecting an establishment of religion, or prohibiting the free exercise thereof; or abridging the freedom of speech, or of the press; or the right of the people peaceably to assemble, and to petition the Government for a redress of grievances.

Amendment II

A well regulated Militia, being necessary to the security of a free State, the right of the people to keep and bear Arms, shall not be infringed.

Amendment III

No Soldier shall, in time of peace be quartered in any house, without the consent of the Owner, nor in time of war, but in a manner to be prescribed by law.

Amendment IV

The right of the people to be secure in their persons, houses, papers, and effects, against unreasonable searches and seizures, shall not be violated, and no Warrants shall issue, but upon probable cause, supported by Oath or affir-mation, and particularly describing the place to be searched, and the persons or things to be seized.

Amendment V

No person shall be held to answer for a capital, or otherwise infamous crime, unless on a presentment or indictment of a Grand Jury, except in cases arising in the land or naval forces, or in the Militia, when in actual service in time of War or public danger; nor shall any person be subject for the same offence to be twice put in jeopardy of life or limb; nor shall be compelled in any criminal case to be a witness against himself, nor be deprived of life, liberty, or property, without due process of law; nor shall private property be taken for public use, without just compensation.

Amendment VI

In all criminal prosecutions, the accused shall enjoy the right to a speedy and public trial, by an impartial jury of the State and district wherein the crime shall have been committed, which district shall have been previously ascertained by law, and to be informed of the nature and cause of the accusation; to be confronted with the witnesses against him; to have compulsory process for obtaining witnesses in his favor, and to have the Assistance of Counsel for his defence.

Amendment VII

In Suits at common law, where the value in controversy shall exceed twenty dollars, the right of trial by jury shall be preserved, and no fact tried by a jury, shall be otherwise re-examined in any Court of the United States, than according to the rules of the common law.

Amendment VIII

Excessive bail shall not be required, nor excessive fines imposed, nor cruel and unusual punishments inflicted.

Amendment IX

The enumeration in the Constitution, of certain rights, shall not be construed to deny or disparage others retained by the people.

Amendment X

The powers not delegated to the United States by the Constitution, nor prohibited by it to the States, are reserved to the States respectively, or to the people.

AMENDMENT XI

Passed by Congress March 4, 1794. Ratified February 7, 1795.

Note: Article III, section 2, of the Constitution was modified by amendment 11.

The Judicial power of the United States shall not be construed to extend to any suit in law or equity, commenced or prosecuted against one of the United States by Citizens of another State, or by Citizens or Subjects of any Foreign State.

AMENDMENT XII

Passed by Congress December 9, 1803. Ratified June 15, 1804.

Note: A portion of Article II, section 1 of the Constitution was superseded by the 12th amendment.

The Electors shall meet in their respective states and vote by ballot for President and Vice-President, one of whom, at least, shall not be an inhabitant of the same state with themselves; they shall name in their ballots the person voted for as President, and in distinct ballots the person voted for as Vice-President, and they shall make distinct lists of all persons voted for as President, and of all persons voted for as Vice-President, and of the number of votes for each, which lists they shall sign and certify, and transmit sealed to the seat of the government of the United States, directed to the President of the Senate; — the President of the Senate shall, in the presence of the Senate and House of Representatives, open all the certificates and the votes shall then be counted; — The person having the greatest number of votes for President, shall be the President, if such number be a majority of the whole number of Electors appointed; and if no person have such majority, then from the persons having the highest numbers not exceeding three on the list of those voted for as President, the House of Representatives shall choose immediately, by ballot, the President. But in choosing the President, the votes shall be taken by states, the representation from each state having one vote; a quorum for this purpose shall consist of a member or members from two-thirds of the states, and a majority of all the states shall be necessary to a choice. [And if the House of Representatives shall not choose a President whenever the right of choice shall devolve upon them, before the fourth day of March next following, then the Vice-President shall act as President, as in case of the death or other constitutional disability of the President. —]*The person having the greatest number of votes as Vice-President, shall be the Vice-President, if such number be a majority of the whole number of Electors appointed, and if no person have a majority, then from the two highest numbers on the list, the Senate shall choose the Vice-President; a quorum for the purpose shall consist of two-thirds of the whole number of Senators, and a majority of the whole number shall be necessary to a choice. But no person constitutionally ineligible to the office of President shall be eligible to that of Vice-President of the United States.

*Superseded by section 3 of the 20th amendment.

AMENDMENT XIII

Passed by Congress January 31, 1865. Ratified December 6, 1865.

Note: A portion of Article IV, section 2, of the Constitution was superseded by the 13th amendment.

Section 1.
Neither slavery nor involuntary servitude, except as a punishment for crime whereof the party shall have been duly convicted, shall exist within the United States, or any place subject to their jurisdiction.

Section 2.
Congress shall have power to enforce this article by appropriate legislation.

AMENDMENT XIV

Passed by Congress June 13, 1866. Ratified July 9, 1868.

Note:Article I, section 2, of the Constitution was modified by section 2 of the 14th amendment.

Section 1.

All persons born or naturalized in the United States, and subject to the jurisdiction thereof, are citizens of the United States and of the State wherein they reside. No State shall make or enforce any law which shall abridge the privileges or immunities of citizens of the United States; nor shall any State deprive any person of life, liberty, or property, without due process of law; nor deny to any person within its jurisdiction the equal protection of the laws.

Section 2.

Representatives shall be apportioned among the several States according to their respective numbers, counting the whole number of persons in each State, excluding Indians not taxed. But when the right to vote at any election for the choice of electors for President and Vice-President of the United States, Representatives in Congress, the Executive and Judicial officers of a State, or the members of the Legislature thereof, is denied to any of the male inhabitants of such State, being twenty-one years of age,* and citizens of the United States, or in any way abridged, except for participation in rebellion, or other crime, the basis of representation therein shall be reduced in the proportion which the number of such male citizens shall bear to the whole number of male citizens twenty-one years of age in such State.

Section 3.

No person shall be a Senator or Representative in Congress, or elector of President and Vice-President, or hold any office, civil or military, under the United States, or under any State, who, having previously taken an oath, as a member of Congress, or as an officer of the United States, or as a mem-

ber of any State legislature, or as an executive or judicial officer of any State, to support the Constitution of the United
States, shall have engaged in insurrection or rebellion against
the same, or given aid or comfort to the enemies thereof. But
Congress may by a vote of two-thirds of each House, remove
such disability.

Section 4.
The validity of the public debt of the United States, authorized by law, including debts incurred for payment of pen-
sions and bounties for services in suppressing insurrection
or rebellion, shall not be questioned. But neither the United
States nor any State shall assume or pay any debt or obligation incurred in aid of insurrection or rebellion against the
United States, or any claim for the loss or emancipation of
any slave; but all such debts, obligations and claims shall be
held illegal and void.

Section 5.
The Congress shall have the power to enforce, by appropriate legislation, the provisions of this article.

Changed by section 1 of the 26th amendment.

AMENDMENT XV

*Passed by Congress February 26, 1869. Ratified February
3, 1870.*

Section 1.
The right of citizens of the United States to vote shall not be
denied or abridged by the United States or by any State on
account of race, color, or previous condition of servitude—

Section 2.
The Congress shall have the power to enforce this article by
appropriate legislation.

AMENDMENT XVI

Passed by Congress July 2, 1909. Ratified February 3, 1913.

Note: Article I, section 9, of the Constitution was modified by amendment 16.

The Congress shall have power to lay and collect taxes on incomes, from whatever source derived, without apportionment among the several States, and without regard to any census or enumeration.

AMENDMENT XVII

Passed by Congress May 13, 1912. Ratified April 8, 1913.

Note: Article I, section 3, of the Constitution was modified by the 17th amendment.

The Senate of the United States shall be composed of two Senators from each State, elected by the people thereof, for six years; and each Senator shall have one vote. The electors in each State shall have the qualifications requisite for electors of the most numerous branch of the State legislatures.

When vacancies happen in the representation of any State in the Senate, the executive authority of such State shall issue writs of election to fill such vacancies: *Provided,* That the legislature of any State may empower the executive thereof to make temporary appointments until the people fill the vacancies by election as the legislature may direct.

This amendment shall not be so construed as to affect the election or term of any Senator chosen before it becomes valid as part of the Constitution.

AMENDMENT XVIII

Passed by Congress December 18, 1917. Ratified January 16, 1919. Repealed by Amendment 21.

Section 1.

After one year from the ratification of this article the manufacture, sale, or transportation of intoxicating liquors within, the importation thereof into, or the exportation thereof from the United States and all territory subject to the jurisdiction thereof for beverage purposes is hereby prohibited.

Section 2.

The Congress and the several States shall have concurrent power to enforce this article by appropriate legislation.

Section 3.

This article shall be inoperative unless it shall have been ratified as an amendment to the Constitution by the legislatures of the several States, as provided in the Constitution, within seven years from the date of the submission hereof to the States by the Congress.

AMENDMENT XIX

Passed by Congress June 4, 1919. Ratified August 18, 1920.

The right of citizens of the United States to vote shall not be denied or abridged by the United States or by any State on account of sex.

Congress shall have power to enforce this article by appropriate legislation.

AMENDMENT XX

Passed by Congress March 2, 1932. Ratified January 23, 1933.

Note: Article I, section 4, of the Constitution was modified by section 2 of this amendment. In addition, a portion of the 12th amendment was superseded by section 3.

Section 1.

The terms of the President and the Vice President shall end at noon on the 20th day of January, and the terms of Senators and Representatives at noon on the 3rd day of January, of the years in which such terms would have ended if this article had not been ratified; and the terms of their successors shall then begin.

Section 2.
The Congress shall assemble at least once in every year, and such meeting shall begin at noon on the 3d day of January, unless they shall by law appoint a different day.

Section 3.
If, at the time fixed for the beginning of the term of the President, the President elect shall have died, the Vice President elect shall become President. If a President shall not have been chosen before the time fixed for the beginning of his term, or if the President elect shall have failed to qualify, then the Vice President elect shall act as President until a President shall have qualified; and the Congress may by law provide for the case wherein neither a President elect nor a Vice President shall have qualified, declaring who shall then act as President, or the manner in which one who is to act shall be selected, and such person shall act accordingly until a President or Vice President shall have qualified.

Section 4.
The Congress may by law provide for the case of the death of any of the persons from whom the House of Representatives may choose a President whenever the right of choice shall have devolved upon them, and for the case of the death of any of the persons from whom the Senate may choose a Vice President whenever the right of choice shall have devolved upon them.

Section 5.
Sections 1 and 2 shall take effect on the 15th day of October following the ratification of this article.

Section 6.
This article shall be inoperative unless it shall have been

ratified as an amendment to the Constitution by the legislatures of three-fourths of the several States within seven years from the date of its submission.

AMENDMENT XXI

Passed by Congress February 20, 1933. Ratified December 5, 1933.

Section 1.
The eighteenth article of amendment to the Constitution of the United States is hereby repealed.

Section 2.
The transportation or importation into any State, Territory, or Possession of the United States for delivery or use therein of intoxicating liquors, in violation of the laws thereof, is hereby prohibited.

Section 3.
This article shall be inoperative unless it shall have been ratified as an amendment to the Constitution by conventions in the several States, as provided in the Constitution, within seven years from the date of the submission hereof to the States by the Congress.

AMENDMENT XXII

Passed by Congress March 21, 1947. Ratified February 27, 1951.

Section 1.
No person shall be elected to the office of the President more than twice, and no person who has held the office of President, or acted as President, for more than two years of a term to which some other person was elected President shall be elected to the office of President more than once. But this Article shall not apply to any person holding the office of President when this Article was proposed by Con-

gress, and shall not prevent any person who may be holding the office of President, or acting as President, during the term within which this Article becomes operative from holding the office of President or acting as President during the remainder of such term.

Section 2.
This article shall be inoperative unless it shall have been ratified as an amendment to the Constitution by the legislatures of three-fourths of the several States within seven years from the date of its submission to the States by the Congress.

AMENDMENT XXIII

Passed by Congress June 16, 1960. Ratified March 29, 1961.

Section 1.
The District constituting the seat of Government of the United States shall appoint in such manner as Congress may direct:

A number of electors of President and Vice President equal to the whole number of Senators and Representatives in Congress to which the District would be entitled if it were a State, but in no event more than the least populous State; they shall be in addition to those appointed by the States, but they shall be considered, for the purposes of the election of President and Vice President, to be electors appointed by a State; and they shall meet in the District and perform such duties as provided by the twelfth article of amendment.

Section 2.
The Congress shall have power to enforce this article by appropriate legislation.

AMENDMENT XXIV

Passed by Congress August 27, 1962. Ratified January 23, 1964.

Section 1.
The right of citizens of the United States to vote in any primary or other election for President or Vice President, for electors for President or Vice President, or for Senator or Representative in Congress, shall not be denied or abridged by the United States or any State by reason of failure to pay poll tax or other tax.

Section 2.
The Congress shall have power to enforce this article by appropriate legislation.

AMENDMENT XXV

Passed by Congress July 6, 1965. Ratified February 10, 1967.

Note: Article II, section 1, of the Constitution was affected by the 25th amendment.

Section 1.
In case of the removal of the President from office or of his death or resignation, the Vice President shall become President.

Section 2.
Whenever there is a vacancy in the office of the Vice President, the President shall nominate a Vice President who shall take office upon confirmation by a majority vote of both Houses of Congress.

Section 3.
Whenever the President transmits to the President pro tempore of the Senate and the Speaker of the House of Representatives his written declaration that he is unable to

discharge the powers and duties of his office, and until he transmits to them a written declaration to the contrary, such powers and duties shall be discharged by the Vice President as Acting President.

Section 4.

Whenever the Vice President and a majority of either the principal officers of the executive departments or of such other body as Congress may by law provide, transmit to the President pro tempore of the Senate and the Speaker of the House of Representatives their written declaration that the President is unable to discharge the powers and duties of his office, the Vice President shall immediately assume the powers and duties of the office as Acting President.

Thereafter, when the President transmits to the President pro tempore of the Senate and the Speaker of the House of Representatives his written declaration that no inability exists, he shall resume the powers and duties of his office unless the Vice President and a majority of either the principal officers of the executive department or of such other body as Congress may by law provide, transmit within four days to the President pro tempore of the Senate and the Speaker of the House of Representatives their written declaration that the President is unable to discharge the powers and duties of his office. Thereupon Congress shall decide the issue, assembling within forty-eight hours for that purpose if not in session. If the Congress, within twenty-one days after receipt of the latter written declaration, or, if Congress is not in session, within twenty-one days after Congress is required to assemble, determines by two-thirds vote of both Houses that the President is unable to discharge the powers and duties of his office, the Vice President shall continue to discharge the same as Acting President; otherwise, the President shall resume the powers and duties of his office.

AMENDMENT XXVI

Passed by Congress March 23, 1971. Ratified July 1, 1971.

Note:Amendment 14, section 2, of the Constitution was modified by section 1 of the 26th amendment.

Section 1.
The right of citizens of the United States, who are eighteen years of age or older, to vote shall not be denied or abridged by the United States or by any State on account of age.

Section 2.
The Congress shall have power to enforce this article by appropriate legislation.

AMENDMENT XXVII

Originally proposed Sept. 25, 1789. Ratified May 7, 1992.

No law, varying the compensation for the services of the Senators and Representatives, shall take effect, until an election of representatives shall have intervened.

Appendix D:
Casualties of the Revolutionary War

Date	Engagement	Commander	Troops	Killed	Wounded	Cap-tured
Apr. 19, 1775	Lexington/ Concord	American: Capt. John Parker, et al	3,763	49	41	0
		British: Lt. Col. Francis Smith	1,800	73	174	7
June 17, 1775	Bunker (Breed's) Hill	American: Gens. Putnam & Ward	2,000	140	271	30
		British: General William Howe	2,400	226	826	0
Sep-Nov 1775	Siege of St.John's	American: Gen. Richard Montgomery	1,500	?	?	?
		British: Major John Preston	720			720
Oct. 15, 1775	Montreal	American: Col. Ethan Allen	110	?	?	40
		British: Gen. Guy Carleton	235	?	?	0
Dec. 9, 1775	Great Bridge	American: Gen. William Woolford	1,000	0	1	0
		British: Lord Dunsmore	600	62*		?
Dec. 31, 1775	Quebec	American: Gen. Richard Montgomery	800	60*		460
		British: Gen. Guy Carleton	1,800	5	13	0
Feb. 27, 1776	Moore's Creek	American: Col. Richard Caswell	1000	1	1	0
		British: Col Donald McLeon	1,780	30*		850
May 15, 1776	The Cedars	American: Maj. Issac Butterfield	540	0	0	400
		British: Capt. Foster	640	?	8	13
June 8, 1776	Trois Rivieres	American: Gen. William Thompson	2,000	160*		236
		British: Gen. Guy Carleton	6,000	8	9	0

* killed and/or wounded   ** wounded and/or captured

Date	Engagement	Commander	Troops	Killed	Wounded	Cap-tured
June 28, 1776	Fort Sullivan	American Gen. William Moultrie	435	17	20	0
		British: Gen. Henry Clinton	9 ships	64	131	0
Aug.27, 1776	Long Island	American: Gen. George Washington	19,000	300	1,100**	
		British: Gen. William Howe	32,000	63	314	23
Sept. 15,1776	Kips Bay	American: Col.William Douglas	900	60*		320
		British: Gen. William Howe	4,000	12*		0
Sept 16, 1776	Harlem Heights	American: Gen. George Washington	2,000	30	100	0
		British: Gen. Alexander Leslie	5,000	14	157	0
Oct. 11, 1776	Valcour Island	American: Col. Benedict Arnold	750	60*		320
		British: Gen. Guy Carleton	1,670	40*		0
Oct. 18, 1776	Pell's Point	American: Col. John Glover	750	8	13	0
		British: Gen. William Howe	4,000	25*		0
Oct. 22, 1776	Mamaroneck	American: Col John Haslet	750	3	12	0
		British: Maj. Robert Rogers	428	77*		36
Oct. 26, 1776	White Plains	American: Gen. George Washington	14,500	28	126	0
		British: Gen. William Howe	14,000	313*		0
Nov. 16, 1776	Fort Washington	American: Col. Robert Magaw	2,967	53	96	2,818
		British: Gen. Baron W. Knyphausen	8,000	78	374	0
Dec. 26, 1776	Trenton	American: Gen. George Washington	2,400	0	4	0
		British: Col. Johann Rall	1,400	22	92	948

Date	Engagement	Commander	Troops	Killed	Wounded	Cap-tured
Jan. 3, 1777	Princeton	American: Gen. George Washington	4,000	30	75	0
		British: Lt. Col. Charles Mawhood	1,200	60	150	244
Jan. 3, 1777	Princeton	American: Gen. George Washington	4,000	30	75	0
		British: Lt. Col. Charles Mawhood	1,200	60	150	244
Apr. 27, 1777	Danbury Raid	American: Col. Benedict Arnold	700	20	80	0
		British: Gov. William Tryon	2,000	154*		40
June 16, 1777	Metuchen	American: Gen. Lord Sterling	2,200	12	50	50
		British: Gen. Charles Cornwallis	4,000	70*		0
July 7, 1777	Hubbardton	American: Col. Henry Van Rensselaer	730	41	95	234
		British: Gen. Baron Freidrich Riedesel	1,030	60	148	0
July 8, 1777	Fort Ann	American: Col. Peter Gansvoort	550	77	23	6
		British: Lt. Col. John Hill	190	13	23	15
Aug. 2, 1777	Fort Stanwix	American: Col. Peter Gansvoort	750	12	23	0
		British: Lt. Col. Barry St. Leger	1,875	?	?	?
Aug. 5, 1777	Oriskany	American: Col. Nicholas Herkimer	5,860	200*		0
		British: Col. John Butler	1,000	150*		
Aug. 16, 1777	Bennington	American: Gen. John Stark	2,330	30	50	0
		British:Lt. Col. Breyman	1,442	207	?	700
Aug. 22, 1777	Staten Island	American: Gen. John Sullivan	1,000	10	15	40
		British: Gen. John Campbell	3,000	?	?	259

* **killed and/or wounded**   ** **wounded and/or captured**

Date	Engagement	Commander	Troops	Killed	Wounded	Cap-tured
Sept. 3, 1777	Cooch's Bridge	American: Gen. William Maxwell	720	40*		0
		British: Lt. Col. Ludwig von Wurm	?	4	5	0
Sept. 11, 1777	Brandywine	American: Gen. George Washington	11,000	1,300*		400
		British: Gen. William Howe	12,500	90	400	0
Sept. 19, 1777	Freeman's Farm	American: Gen. Horatio Gates	7,000	65	218	0
		British: Gen. John Burgoyne	6,000	600*		0
Sept. 21, 1777	Paoli	American: Gen. Anthony Wayne	1,500	150*		17
		British: Gen. Charles Grey	?	4	5	0
Oct. 4, 1777	Germantown	American: Gen. George Washington	11,000	152	521	400
		British: Gen. William Howe	9,000	70	400	14
Oct. 6, 1777	Fort Montgomery	Gen. George Clinton	600	25*		227
		Gen. Henry Clinton	3,000	40	150	0
Oct 7, 1777	Saratoga	American: Gen. Horatio Gates	11,000	50	150	0
		British: Gen. John Burgoyne	6,300	600*		5,300
Oct. 22, 1777	Fort Mercer	American: Gen. Nathaniel Greene	400	14	23	0
		British: Col. Carl von Donop	1,200	377*		20
Nov. 10, 1777	Port Mifflin	American: Lt. Col. Samuel Smith	450	250*		227
		British: Gen. William Howe	?	13	24	0
Dec. 5, 1777	White Marsh		11,000	90*		0
		British: Gen. William Howe	14,000	60*		0

Date	Engagement	Commander	Troops	Killed	Wounded	Cap-tured
Jan. 28, 1778	Monmouth Court House	American: Gen. George Washington	13,425	152	300	37
		British: Gen. Sir Henry Clinton	13,000	190	390	576
July 3, 1778	Wyoming	American: Col. Zebulon Butler	360	300		0
		British: Col. John Butler	900	3	8	0
Aug. 29, 1778	Newport	American: Gen. John Sullivan	5,000	30	137	0
		British: Gen. Sir Robert Pigot	3,000	38	210	0
Nov. 11, 1778	Cherry Valley	American: Col. Ichabod Alden	250	70*		71
		British: Walter Butler/Joseph Brnat	700	?	?	0
Dec. 29, 1778	Savannah	American: Gen. Robert Howe	850	83*		453
		British: Lt. Col. Archibald Campbell	3,500	3	10	0
Feb 3, 1779	Beaufort	American: Gen. William Moultrie	320	8	23	0
		British: Major Gardiner	200	?	?	0
Feb 14, 1779	Kettle Creek	American: Col. Andrew Pickins	300	9	23	0
		British: Col. Boyd	400	40*		70
Mar. 3, 1779	Briar Creek	American: Gen. John Ashe	1,700	200*		173
		British: Lt. Col. Mark Provost	900	5	11	0
June 20, 1779	Stono Ferry	American: Gen. Benjamin Lincoln	1,200	146*		
		British: Lt. Col. John Maitland	900	26	103	0
July 16, 1779	Stoney Point	American: Gen. Anthony Wayne	1,350	15	83	0
		British: Lt. Col. Henry Johnson	625	20	74	574

* killed and/or wounded   ** wounded and/or captured

Date	Engagement	Commander	Troops	Killed	Wounded	Captured
Jul/Aug 1779	Penobscot	American: Gen. Lovell/Gen.Wadsworth	1,000	474* **		
		British: Col. Francis McLean	600	13*		0
Aug. 19, 1779	Paulus Hook	American: Col. Henry Lee	300	2	3	
		British: Maj. William Sutherland	250	50*		158
Aug. 29, 1779	Newtown	American: Gen. John Sutherland	3,462	3	39	0
		British: Walter Butler/Joseph Brant	1,200	12*		0
Sept. 16, 1779	Siege of Savannah	American: Gen. Benjamin Lincoln	5,050	244	584	0
		British: Gen. Augus-tine Prevost	3,200	40	63	
Feb. 3, 1780	Youngs House	American: Lt. Col. Joseph Thompson	1,025	12	60	0
		British: Lt. Col. Chapple Newton	550	5	18	0
Mar. 29, 1780	Siege of Charleston	American: Gen. Benjamin Lincolm	5,000	92	148	4,650
		British: Gen. Sir Henry Clinton	14,000	76	189	0
Apr. 14, 1780	Monck's Corner	American: Gen. Isaac Huger	500	20*		67
		British: Lt. Col. Banastre Tarlton	650	0	3	0
May 6, 1780	Lenud's Ferry	American: Col. William Washington	350	41*		67
		British: Lt. Col. Banastre Tarlton	150	7	7	?
May 29, 1780	Waxhaws	American: Col Abraham Buford	400	113	200**	
		British: Lt. Col. Banastre Tarlton	270	5	15	?
June 7-23, 1780	Springfield	American: Gen. Nathaniel Greene	1,800	15	61	0
		British: Gen. W. Knyphausen	5,000	150*		0

Date	Engagement	Commander	Troops	Killed	Wounded	Captured
June 20, 1780	Ramseur's Mill	American: Col. Frances Locke	400	150*		0
		British: Lt. Col John Moore	1300	150*		0
June 20, 1780	Ramseur's Mill	American: Col. Frances Locke	400	150*		0
		British: Lt. Col John Moore	1300	150*		0
Aug. 1, 1780	Rocky Mount	American: Col. Thomas Sumter	600	14*		0
		British: Lt. Col George Turnbull	500	20*		0
Aug. 16, 1780	Camden	American: Gen. Horatio Gates	3,052	1,050**		
		British: Gen. Lord Charles Cornwallis	2,239	68	245	0
Aug 18,. 1780	Fishing Creek	American: Col. Thomas Sumter	700	150*		330
		British: Lt. Col. Banastre Tarlton	160	16*		0
Oct. 7, 1780	Kings Mountain	American: Col. Wm. Campbell, et al	900	28	62	0
		British: Maj. Patrick Ferguson	1,000	157	163	698
Oct. 19, 1780	Klock's Field	American: Gen. Robert Van Rensselaer	1,500	?	?	?
		British: Sir John Johnson	1,000	?	?	?
Nov. 20, 1780	Blackstock's Plantation	American: Col. Thomas Sumter	1,000	3	5	0
		British: Lt. Col. Banastre Tarlton	270	50*		0
Jan. 17, 1781	Cowpens	American: Gen. Daniel Morgan	1,025	12	60	0
		British: Lt. Col. Banastre Tarlton	1,100	100	229	829
Feb. 25, 1781	Haw River	American: Cols. Pickens and Lee	600	0	0	0
		British: Col. John Pyle	400	90	250	0

* killed and/or wounded   ** wounded and/or captured

Date	Engagement	Commander	Troops	Killed	Wounded	Cap-tured
Mar. 6, 1781	Wetzell's Mill	American: Col. Otho Williams	700	20*		0
		British: Lt. Col. Banastre Tarlton	1,200	21*		0
Mar. 15, 1781	Guilford Court House	American: Gen. Nathaniel Greene	4,400	78	183	0
		British: Gen. Lord Charles Cornwallis	1,900	143	389	?
Apr. 25, 1781	Blandford	American: Gen. Baron A. von Steuben	1,000	60*		0
		British: Gen. William Phillips	2,500	70*		?
Apr. 25, 1781	Hobkirk's Hill	American: Gen. Nathaniel Greene	1,551	19	115	0
		British: Lt. Col. Lord Francis Rawdon	900	38	190	50
May 8, 1781	Fort Motte	American: Gen. Francis Marion	450	2	0	0
		British: Lt. Donald McPherson	175			175
May 22, 1781	Siege of Augusta	American: Gen. Andrew Pickens	1,600	16	35	0
		British: Lt. Col. Thomas Browne	630	52*		334
May 22, 1781	Siege of Ninety-Six	American: Gen. Nathaniel Greene	1,500	57	70	0
		British: Lt. Col. Cruger	550	27	58	
June 26, 1781	Spencer's Ordinary	American: Col. Richard Butler	570	9	14	32
		British: Lt. Col. John Simcoe	400	10	23	0
July 6, 1781	Greenspring Farm	American: Gens. LaFayette and A. Wayne	900	28	99	12
		British: Gen. Lord Charles Cornwallis	7,000	75*		0
Sept.6, 1781	Groton Heights (Fort Griswold)	American:Cmdr. William Ledyard	150	83	39 **	
		British: Gen. Benedict Arnold	800	52	144	0

Date	Engagement	Commander	Troops	Killed	Wounded	Captured
Sept.6, 1781	Burning of New London	American:Cmdr. William Ledyard	150	6	20	
		British: Gen. Benedict Arnold	800	6	20	0
Sept. 8, 1781	Eutaw Springs	American: Gen. Nathaniel Greene	2,200	139	365	0
		British: Lt. Col. Alexander Stewart	2,000	85	351	400
Sept. 12, 1781	Cane Creek	American: Col. John Butler	400	25	90	10
		British: Cols. D. Fanning & H. McNeil	950	27	90	0
Sept. 28, 1781	Siege of Yorktown	American: Gen. George Washington & Gen. Comte Rochambeau	11,133 7,800	23 60	65 193	0 0
		British: Gen. Lord Charles Cornwallis	8,885	156	326	8,087

* killed and/or wounded   ** wounded and/or captured

Acknowledgements

I have so many people to thank for making this work possible. In the fight for liberty, one is pulled in numerous directions. And while I have often felt stretched beyond measure, so many individuals made sure that this important work, that I hope will facilitate restoration in America, came to a "near-perfect" completion.

To my wife, Janelle, for her unwavering support, love, and motivation to stand strong in the midst of the unsettling storm. She is my best friend and my companion who pushes me to engage in the struggle for freedom and sees on the horizon what I often miss. She has the tenderness of Martha Washington, the vigor of Abigail Adams, and the fight and determination of Emily Geiger. She will certainly be a lady who will be remembered for her belief, faith, and love.

To my children, who pushed me to awaken Americans to their duty to defend the great American experiment. They constantly remind of the realization that a few committed people can make a difference. Ammon, Daniel, Jacob, Fenton, Aidan, and Shanelle mean the world to me, and this fight today is to preserve their freedom tomorrow. May they dedicate their lives to the cause of preserving what is fundamentally their birthright, namely freedom.

To my mother, Erna Arnold, who does what great mothers do—supports, encourages, and protects. As an immigrant from Switzerland, she taught me many of the principles found in this book, and it is my honor to pass on this important knowledge.

To Garry Johnson, Aaron Mackley, Keith Buchanan, and Don Petrie, all of whom kept me on track and made sure that this work was fashioned in a way that would facilitate a meeting with the current culture at the "table of relevance." Their incredible vision of addressing the needs of America has been awe-inspiring and, often times, jaw-dropping. Such men of this caliber, without question, surrounded some of the greatest leaders in America's history.

To Robbie and Lisa Barrkman, both of whom have been two of my greatest supporters. Their love of America is unmatched and their desire to repair America is unrelenting. If you want to know what real colonial soldiers looked like, all one needs to do is sit down with Robbie and Lisa and you will experience dedication to the greatest cause the world has ever known. Their fire is contagious and their love of country reignites me with each passing conversation.

To Evelyn Dennis, who is the backbone behind much of my work. She has coordinated, motivated, and worked endless hours to help me move the message. She worked tirelessly to ensure that I was able to complete a product she always made clear could "change the culture of America."

To William "Bill" Bish, who has been by my side in this battle from almost the beginning. He is the friend that I've always dreamed of. He is the man who has pushed me and constructively criticized me when no one else was watching, and he stood, motivated, smiled, laughed, and cried when everyone could see. Few will ever know of our disagreements. Everyone will know of our mutual love for each other and America. He is truly an asset to this country.

To the tens of thousands of people who have heard me speak, motivated me to continue on, and opened countless doors to spread the message of more freedom and less government. Thank you for inspiring me to complete this work that America so desperately needs. Without you on my side, there is no real fight that has hope.

About the Author

Shane F. Krauser is the director of the American Academy for Constitutional Education (AAFCE), an adjunct professor of constitutional and criminal law, a radio talk show host, a firearms instructor, and an experienced trial attorney. He has written extensively on the principles of freedom and the Constitution.

Shane completed his undergraduate work at Arizona State University in 1996, where he graduated *summa cum laude*. Shortly thereafter in 2001, he graduated with his law degree (JD) from the University of Utah.

Shane has been involved in numerous projects of constitutional import, including the Oklahoma City Bombing Trial, victims' rights legislation, and an attempt to overturn the Fifth Amendment's Miranda requirements argued before the U.S. Supreme Court (*Dickerson v. United States*). He has also worked as a felony prosecutor in Arizona, where he handled cases involving gang violence, homicide, armed robbery, aggravated assault, and home invasions. Shane has also worked as a criminal defense attorney and a litigator and consultant on cases implicating the Constitution.

Shane was born and raised in Arizona. He grew up in a family where the principles of human freedom and the exceptionalism of America were often debated and discussed. He has focused on carrying this tradition forward with his own family, as he recognizes the strength of this country lies in its youth and their understanding of liberty and history.

Shane and his beautiful wife, Janelle, are the parents of six children. They reside in Arizona, where they enjoy traveling, the outdoors, and being involved together in the fight for freedom.

Contact

FOR BOOK SALES, SPEAKING ENGAGEMENTS, AND SEMINARS

Shane Krauser is a widely sought-after speaker, has traveled the country speaking on countless issues pertaining to the Constitution and human freedom, and has been called by many "the best instructor of the Constitution in the country."

He has spoken at political rallies, addressed large audiences at various political and corporate conventions, guided expert panels with various national figures, appeared on national radio and TV, inspired students in both public and private schools, presented at numerous colleges and universities, and educated audiences of all sizes and demographics. He brings a wealth of knowledge to any forum, and that knowledge will inspire you. His experiences will captivate you. His dedication will move you.

Shane has worked directly with members of U.S. Congress and the various state legislatures on various pieces of legislation with an emphatic focus on the Constitution. He has also spent significant time helping mobilize and promote the cause of freedom with many grassroots organizations all over America.

One of the core problems in America is that so many do not know what it means to be an American. Shane goes right to the core of the issue and will convince you in your heart and mind that America is exceptional in more ways than one, and that now is the time to stand up and defend her.

Shane is available to speak at any number of venues and may be contacted at info@ShaneKrauser.com. To order books, contact info@ShaneKrauser.com or go towww.ShaneKrauser.com.